"In *Sharing Faith Online*, Sean Salai has pro... valuable resource to those seeking to share the Good News of Jesus Christ. The digital revolution caught the Church off-guard. The pandemic further heightened the unexpected need for the Church to have a digital presence. Now, in this easy-to-read volume, we have a field manual on how the Church can get ahead of the curve and have a robust--rather than merely reactionary--digital presence and plan for evangelization online."

Fr. Jeff Kirby, STD, *Crux* senior contributor

"The internet offers unprecedented opportunities to spread both truth and utter nonsense, the gospel and rumors only a fool would believe. Sean Salai gives us a useful guide to navigating and deploying the tools of the New Media for the purposes of Christ while defusing the evils that poison on-line discourse. Bravo!"

Mark P. Shea, Catholic blogger and author

"As a lawyer and as an educator, I know that the means of communication often is vitally important to the successful conveyance of ideas. In *Sharing Faith Online*, Sean Salai, SJ, shows how to use new messaging to present eternal truths effectively. It is an important book."

Ronald J. Rychlak, Distinguished Professor of Law, The University of Mississippi

"Sean Salai, SJ, has taken on two looming tasks for the Church: the generational issues in religious practice and the potential of social media to accomplish part of what the Church needs to accomplish today. He led a large group of people through the Spiritual Exercises of St. Ignatius; he did so with a particular focus on contemporary needs. From his study of the participants who persevered through the experience and gave concrete feedback, Salai offers some concrete directions for outreach over social media for believers today."

Frank DeSiano, CSP, President,
Paulist Evangelization Ministries

"Online spirituality is an urgent topic in the wake of the pandemic and amid the decline of institutional religion in America. Salai's unique combination of ecclesial and journalistic background qualifies him to address such issues intelligently."

Mark Tooley, President,
Institute on Religion and Democracy

Some decades ago, Walter Ong alerted us to how communicational technology paradoxically involves external, distancing apparatus even as it facilitates the greater sharing of individuals' interiority. This was true of the invention of writing and it is also true of our internet connections. If people can fall in love via the internet, can faith communities not arise and be sustained through the same mechanism? Sean Salai has given us a carefully organized, experience-based study that opens upon this arena. His work is a doorway to what is sure to be an increasingly important avenue of evangelization and Church life."

Claude Pavur, SJ, Associate Editor, Jesuit Sources

"Today, both preaching and scholarship depend on our use of digital media, as well as on more traditional ways of communicating ideas, to get their message across. Does this change in the tools we use bring about changes in the content or style of the message itself? Sean Salai's new book on the implications for faith and prayer that he discovered in directing the Spiritual Exercises of St. Ignatius on Facebook leads us to a whole new realm of understanding the implications of digital media for evangelization—a sign of the coming of a new age in the communication of God's transforming Word."

Brian Daley, SJ, Emeritus Professor of Theology, University of Notre Dame

"Sean Salai, S.J., brilliantly retains the reader's attention as he sets out possibilities for social media in sharing Christian faith online. His proposals for digital evangelization are rooted in the encounter with Jesus Christ made possible by the Spiritual Exercises of St Ignatius Loyola. A fascinating and valuable book."

Gerald O'Collins, SJ, AC, Professor Emeritus of the Gregorian University, Rome

"Sean Salai reminds us that everyone has a pulpit in their pocket, as close as their cell phone. We need to find ways to make that device shed light — not just heat. His important and penetrating analysis is a welcome look at what the Church needs to do to make that happen and, just maybe, win over a new generation of believers."

Deacon Greg Kandra, blogger, "The Deacon's Bench"

SHARING FAITH ONLINE

SHARING FAITH ONLINE

A Guide to
Digital Evangelization

SEAN SALAI, SJ

New City Press
Hyde Park, New York

Published by New City Press
202 Comforter Blvd.,
Hyde Park, NY 12538
www.newcitypress.com

©2022 New City Press

Sharing the Faith Online
A Guide to Digital Evangelization

Imprimi Potest
Very Rev. Thomas P. Greene, SJ
Provincial, US Central and Southern Jesuit Province
June 4, 2021

*This book is based on a dissertation treatise for the Doctor of Ministry
degree at the Catholic University of America, conferred May 2021,
available on ProQuest under the title "Evangelizing Catholic Media
Consumers in an Online Faith-Sharing Group."*

Cover design and layout by Miguel Tejerina

Library of Congress Control Number: 2022900831

ISBN: 978-1-56548-533-4 (paper)
ISBN: 978-1-56548-534-1 (e-book)

Printed in the United States of America

Contents

Additional background information about the research behind the "Spiritual Exercises Faith-Sharing Retreat Group" is available at **https://www.newcitypress.com/media/downloads/ Sharing_faith_online_Appendix.pdf** where four additional appendices can be found:

Appendix A
Project Technology Plan

Appendix B
Texts of Facebook Messages

Appendix C
Raw Data and Slides
from the Facebook Group

Appendix D
Generational Breakdown
for Key Survey Questions

Introduction

This is not your typical handbook. In this book I want to tell you a story about how the digital revolution has changed our ways of interacting in the world, how it has challenged both secular and faith-based communications to adapt, and what believers can do about it. The unfolding story of social media comprises merely the latest chapter in the story of Christianity's attempts to spread the good news through any means possible, but it has become a particularly urgent passage in the narrative of declining religious affiliation amid this twenty-first century after the birth of our savior. The story I will tell is also, most importantly, the story of ordinary Christians who wade into the muck of social media and wonder: Where is God in all of this?

God, of course, is in you and me. As believers, it falls upon us to make the divine story known and to share our faith in a way that invites people into relationship with us. If those of us who are Christians do not share our faith online effectively, the story of Jesus Christ and his followers will remain unknown or muted in the emerging mission field of new media. But if we enter generously into the stories of this book, making them part of our own stories, we may find the real handbook to online faith-sharing written more on our hearts than in these pages.

Perhaps more than other Christians, Catholics have struggled to create digital spaces of faith-based encounter, and so the story of my own church's efforts to share faith in a digital age will frame this book in a way that hopefully still resonates with other Christians and with people of any religion. Because Catholics have such a formalized body of teaching on mass communications, they provide a helpful case study for trends affecting people of all religions. In the six decades since the Second Vatican Council endorsed the evangelizing potential of traditional mass media in *Inter Mirifica,* successive popes have reaffirmed their value in a growing body of magisterial teaching. Yet the digital revolution that made wireless internet and smartphones commonplace in the early 2010s caused a shift from a packaged to a participatory media culture, where every handheld device user became a potential influencer. Pew Forum surveys from 2014 and 2019 showed US Catholics trailing other Christians in sharing their faith through the new media of social networking that privileges two-way interaction over one-way presentation, creating a pastoral disconnect with young adults who, before doing so offline, encounter religion online at significant levels.

America Media, a Jesuit communications ministry for which I write, has embraced this digital shift by rebranding from a magazine into a web portal with multiple digital platforms. In his documents *Gaudete et Exultate* and *Christus Vivit,* Pope Francis has proposed the pastoral practice of accompaniment as essential to this sort of digital outreach, urging Catholics to build relationships more personally online with young adults who no longer see churchgoing as a cultural norm. Researcher Nancy Baym finds correlations between online interaction and offline social habits like visiting family or friends and having a non-kin confidant. Adapted for online faith-sharing, the *Spiritual Exercises of St. Ignatius of Loyola*[1]

---

1. The *Spiritual Exercises* are available online at http://spex.ignatianspirituality.com/SpiritualExercises/Puhl

suggests a framework to study the quality of these online-offline dynamics.

All of these people and resources will shape the story I am about to tell. That will include telling the more particular story of how I accompanied seventy-four people in a "Spiritual Exercises Faith-Sharing Retreat Group" on Facebook as a pastoral case study for Catholic media to evangelize their consumers through social networking. To create our group, I invited people into a thirty-day retreat experience that followed the four themes of the *Exercises* — to feel contrition for sin, follow Jesus in discipleship, suffer with him in his passion, and rejoice in his resurrection. Unlike many online retreats that simply post videos for passive individual consumption, our group included daily faith-sharing prompts to encourage a sense of community through conversation.

Facilitating this retreat as a private group, I targeted Catholic digital media consumers from existing Ignatian groups on *America's* page and elsewhere. My Doctor of Ministry treatise, the original source text of this book available for download at ProQuest, analyzes more fully the responses to pre- and post-retreat surveys to show the self-reported growth of the participants in relationship with each other, themselves, and God over four seven-day sessions of daily videos. Ultimately, I found that when Christians go beyond individualized viewing of videos to discuss deeper questions in an online group setting, they become more comfortable with spiritual conversation and desire to share faith more deeply both offline and online, a hopeful sign for digital evangelization. In this book, I want to tell their stories within the broader narratives of Catholic and secular communication in a digital age. That's because the point of all faith-sharing remains the dynamic encounter with Jesus Christ and with one another in a community that leads us to greater self-knowledge of our relational connections in a constantly changing world. I hope you too will place yourself in this story as the following pages gently invite you on a deeper journey into this digital age of salvation history, trusting in God's loving desire for you to find connection, peace, and freedom in your relationships both online and offline.

Sean Salai, SJ
October 12, 2021
Feast of Carlo Acutis, Patron Saint of the Internet

Chapter 1

From Packaged to Participatory Communication

When used in an interactive way, social media allows people of all ages to have authentic community over the internet, potentially experiencing spiritual growth and change. All theology—especially pastoral theology—starts in a context of "present human experience."[2] Therefore, I want to begin this story of evangelization understood as "the sharing of faith in Christ"[3] with the story of our present human experiences. This is the story of a rapidly changing digital media world rooted in mid-twentieth century electric technologies.

There is an urgent pastoral reason to share this story more widely among believers. As the mid-twenty-first century approaches, religious evangelizers in a post-coronavirus world face an unavoidable choice with new media: use it effectively or accept the fact of increasing social irrelevance in a digital age. Not-choosing will itself be a choice to avoid engaging what has become a large part of ordinary human relations, especially since the March 2020 Covid-19 shutdown of public liturgies which forced Christians globally to celebrate Holy Week and Easter through videos streamed online, believ-

---

2. Stephen B. Bevans, SVD, *Models of Contextual Theology,* 2nd ed. (Maryknoll: Orbis Books, 2002), 4.
3. Francis Cardinal Arinze, *The Evangelizing Parish* (San Francisco: Ignatius Press, 2018), 16-18.

ers can either rationalize their neglect of social networking or engage it more effectively than in the past. The digital revolution, meanwhile, invites believers to recover and adapt the tools of small-group spirituality to new media as a response to the signs of the times, moving beyond the passive viewing of recorded liturgical celebrations or other religious presentations to building community online. The Ignatian tradition that formed me in particular understands spirituality as a communal deepening of the threefold relationship with God, oneself, and others, rooted in Jesus Christ's great commandment to love God "with all your heart" and "love your neighbor as yourself."[4] In this context, it might finally be said that in a digital age the New Evangelization calls Catholics and other believers to use social networking as a fresh tool in the perennial witness that faith-based community offers to the existential peripheries of an ever-changing world.

The Shift of Digital Media: McLuhan's Insights

While traditional media remain influential insofar as they never entirely disappear, the world continually moves forward into new communications technologies, creating pastoral challenges for faith-based outreach. The digital revolution has transformed electronic mass communication from a sender-receiver media culture of prepackaged monologue (e.g., recorded video lectures, radio advertisements, and mass-produced books) into a two-way participatory culture of dialogue (e.g., posting and discussing videos on social media) unprecedented in human history, inviting believers to embrace a paral-

---

4. Matt 22:36-40 (Unless otherwise noted, all scriptural references are from the New American Bible Revised Edition).

lel shift in how to share the message of Jesus. Understanding "faith-sharing" broadly as any discussion of religious topics or experiences, St. Ignatius of Loyola would have described an online faith-sharing group retreat as an example of "spiritual conversation," a phrase well-suited to the digital revolution. In Ignatian spirituality, this term traditionally covers all grounds of faith-based interaction, as it may connote a conversation in the confessional, informal pastoral counseling, or spiritual direction, in addition to people discussing faith casually.

Marshall McLuhan (1911-1980), a pioneering media scholar and philosopher who also happened to be a Catholic layman, offered us one way to understand the origin story of digital media when more than half a century ago he prophesied this relational dynamism of a socially networked world: "The medium, or process, of our time—electric technology—is reshaping and restructuring patterns of social interdependence and every aspect of our personal life."[5] Penning these words in 1967, McLuhan saw the electric technologies of television, radio, and film as "new media" compared to the "old media" of the printed word, with mobile devices and touch-screen technology then existing only in the science-fiction world of *Star Trek*. As McLuhan elaborated on his bold claim that "we now live in a global village . . . a simultaneous happening" of "instant communication" and "active interplay,"[6] at the Second Vatican Council (1962-1965) the Catholic Church had just committed herself to using this "electric technology" in sharing the message of Jesus through catechesis and preaching. Yet even before the world's bishops saw the potential of

---

5. Marshall McLuhan and Quentin Fiore, *The Medium is the Massage: An Inventory of Effects* (Berkeley: Gingko Press, 1967), 8.
6. McLuhan and Fiore, 63.

mass communications, McLuhan had broadened the definition of "medium" to mean any technological extension of the human body or mind—for example, the stirrup, bicycle, and car as physical protractions of the human foot—that restructures social interaction. As a medium creates roles and renegotiates social norms to match the accelerated processes of the workplace which ensue, people must adapt to keep communicating effectively. In his 1964 *magnum opus*, McLuhan defined his thesis that "the medium is the message" (or the "massage," in his alternate spelling that stresses how "all media work us over completely") as such: "This is merely to say that the personal and social consequences of any medium—that is, of any extension of ourselves—result from the new scale that is introduced into our affairs by each extension of ourselves, or by any new technology."[7]

In McLuhan's narrative, each new human technology, from language itself (the primordial medium) to the internet, creates a revolution that changes how people communicate, with the medium of television representing for him the most significant advance of that time. This restructuring does not make people throw out traditional technology; it just obliges us to keep adding onto existing technologies to function well in an increasingly complex global society. For example, many businesses still use fax machines to send documents, but they would lag behind competitors if they did not also scan them digitally on smart devices.

Simply adding a new technology does not make it effective; human beings must adapt our ways of interacting to its rules. Not all media have equal influence and not all new

---

7. Marshall McLuhan, *Understanding Media: The Extensions of Man,* 3rd ed., ed. W. Terrence Gordon (Berkeley: Gingko Press, 2003), 19.

media find skillful users who employ them effectively with the fresh mindsets they require. McLuhan distinguishes between *packaged technologies* (like a printed catechism) that render people passive consumers of whatever messages the creators program into their brains and *participatory technologies* (like a televised political debate) that engage people's active interaction to transformative effect. In the electric platforms that McLuhan described as "mere packaging devices for consumers"—the now-traditional media of press, film, and radio—social communication remained relatively static compared to television, his prime example of the powerful electronic interdependence people form by sharing experiences across vast distances to feel like conversation partners in an invisible community of likeminded people.[8] (By watching a live televised sports game in team apparel, for example, viewers may feel like an active part of that communal interaction.) While packaged technology silences and isolates consumers in our own minds, participatory technology inspires us to communicate freely, connecting us viscerally through our senses to a larger networked sense of community.

Technology builds up this communal interdependence only to the extent that participants engage it actively: People may use passive technology creatively to interact in an engaged way just as they may use digital technology unimaginatively in an isolating way. In their day printed religious books felt participatory due to the conversations they inspired; over time they only began to seem passive relative to how people came to use them and to later technologies. Judging the participatory nature of a medium by how deeply it engages the physical and intellectual senses, McLuhan contrasts several examples

---

8. McLuhan and Fiore, 125.

of low-participation media (radio, print, photographs, movies, lectures) with their corresponding forms of high-participation media (telephone, speech, cartoons, television, seminars) to illustrate this point. While the low-participation medium of radio produces a high level of information and asks little of users, to take the first pairing, the high-participation medium of the telephone gives little information and asks users to fill in the gaps by speaking as well as listening. Along these lines, a telephone call between two actively engaged people remains objectively more embodied than viewing a cartoon, even as the cartoon remains a more imaginative extension of the human eye than a photograph.

By this logic, internet communication offers the most dynamic and participatory form of media to date: Social networks like Facebook, available instantly on a handheld smart device, allow consumers to project multiple bodily senses (e.g., eyes, ears, hands, face, vocal cords, etc.) in generating our own multimedia content at the touch of a button through a variety of digital communications tools ranging from picture and sound to video and digital art. It creates new possibilities for participants to feel more engaged with religious interaction. By letting participants discuss content rather than simply consume it mentally in their isolated thoughts, social networks like Facebook can easily facilitate interactive processes that foster authentic faith-sharing and even spiritual growth.

This digital revolution of simultaneous global interaction, available at any instant, seems to validate more clearly than ever McLuhan's idea of media as extensions of the human senses (touch, taste, smell, sight, sound) that reshape the pattern, pace, and scale of human relationships. With social media, human relations have attained their most embodied technology yet for real-time global conversation, reshaping people's sense of community and the possibility of communicating religiously in a more intensely interactive way. That makes my Facebook retreat, which drew people from all over the world into an asynchronous faith-sharing group, a timely response to the digital revolution's impact on the religious and social habits of Christians.

Even before the digital revolution, Christians used new media from the very beginning to share their faith by extending their bodily senses technologically. In its earliest days, Christian witness to the word of God began with Jesus forming relationships at dinner tables and hillsides where socially marginal people like tax collectors, the poor, the sick, and prostitutes shared their deepest concerns while listening eagerly to his words. Teaching with an authority people recognized as more personal than positional, this humble carpenter with a rabbi's eloquence established friendships based on attraction rather than compulsion, inviting them with passionate urgency to "come, and you will see" as he shared his unique gift for community at meals and fellowship. [9] After his departure from their midst, the earliest Christians nurtured their faith in Jesus domestically in the context of their families, meeting in private homes (house churches) after the synagogues expelled them and Roman law forbade them to assemble publicly. Soon they used the medium of the written word in letters (epistles) that extended their voices and shared the faith more widely. After Constantine legalized Christianity with the Edict of Milan in AD 313, the early Christians gradually erected parish churches and assembled various papyrus scrolls into the canonical Holy Bible—a collection of sacred writings that be-

---

9. John 1:39.

came fixed into one book—to supplement the oral tradition of reciting holy words and stories from memory.

Seen through McLuhan's lens, Christianity grew through and with the new media that emerged over time, helping unite its disconnected house churches into a global network of believers who considered themselves one faith community. Subsequent centuries introduced technologies ranging from illuminated manuscripts to the electric light bulb, further enhancing opportunities to tell the story of faith in ways that unified Western Christians in parishes and dioceses as well as eventually under the Roman papacy. Just as the early believers developed their house churches into a global communion through the help of the written word, twenty-first-century Christians now have a chance to evangelize through new media, using social networks like Facebook as digital extensions of faith-based communities.

This opportunity for digital forms of community-building outreach has become especially timely in light of data showing that people living in historically Christian nations no longer experience churchgoing as the cultural norm in their families, yet continue to interact with believers all over the globe on social media. In a 2014 study of declining religious observance in Great Britain, Bex Lewis reported that her countrymen increasingly engaged Christian religious conversation online before seeking out offline experiences: "For churches, websites and social networks such as Twitter, Facebook, YouTube and Pinterest have now effectively become the 'front door' to billions of digital users."[10]

---

10. Bex Lewis, "The Digital Age: A Challenge for Christian Discipleship" (unpublished paper, The Proceedings of the European Conference on Social Media, July 1, 2014).

Intergenerational Pastoral Challenges

This migration of people's first encounter with the Christian story from the Sunday family pew to online platforms also holds true in the United States. In 2018 and 2019 telephone surveys of 12,738 Americans, a Pew Research Forum study of religious identity and attendance reported that the number of self-identified Christians among Americans dropped from 77 percent in a 2009 survey of 12,529 people to 65 percent in 2019. In that same ten-year period, the religiously unaffiliated "nones" (people self-reporting as agnostic, atheist, or "nothing in particular") grew from 17 to 26 percent. Self-identified Catholics dropped from 23 to 20 percent of the overall population while for the first time Americans attending religious services a few times a year or less (54 percent) suddenly outnumbered regular attendees (45 percent attending at least monthly). Analyzed generationally, the numbers become even more revealing of communal breakdown, exposing the intergenerational pastoral challenges of a digital age.

While the above trends held true across all races, religions, and regions, the one notable discrepancy occurred across generations, with only 49 percent of Generation Y millennials born 1981-96 identifying as Christians compared to the majority of older generations: 67 percent of Generation X born 1965-80, 76 percent of Baby Boomers born 1946-64, and 84 percent of the Silent Generation born 1928-45.[11] Millennials proved least likely to attend religious services, with equal

---

11. Although this study does not break down millennials into sub-groups, trends like decreased religious affiliation intensify across generations as age decreases, making the oldest millennials born in 1981 likelier to self-identify as Christians than the youngest born in 1996. The same holds for religious observance.

number who never attend (22 percent) or attend weekly (22 percent), and 64 percent who attend only "a few times a year" or less often. While the same 62 percent of self-identified Christians across all generations attended religious services at least monthly in 2019 as did in 2009, Pew noted practicing Christians shrinking as an overall segment of the population: "While the trends are clear–the US is steadily becoming less Christian and less religiously observant as the share of adults who are not religious grows–self-described Christians report that they attend religious services at about the same rate today as in 2009."[12]

Even as young Americans increasingly grow up without attending church, additional Pew findings confirm that when they encounter faith-based witness at all, they do so online, illuminating an area of outreach where Catholics lag behind other Christians. A Pew religion and electronic media survey of 3,217 US adults in May and June of 2014 found 20 percent of them sharing their religious faith online in an average week—roughly the same number as watched religious television, listened to religious talk radio, or listened to Christian rock—and 46 percent seeing others share "something about their religious faith" online. Millennials, then aged 18-29, proved twice as likely to encounter online faith-sharing as Americans older than 50, who proved likelier to watch religious television than Americans under 30 at that time. White evangelicals and black Protestants proved likeliest to share their faith both offline and online, with Catholics being third-likeliest (38 percent) after them to share in person and tying for least likely (15 percent) of five Christian faith

---

12. Pew Research Center, Oct. 17, 2019, "In U.S., Decline of Christianity Continues at Rapid Pace."

groups to share online. Underlining the problematic nature of this statistic for Catholics who wish to engage young people, Pew noted a link between online faith-sharing participation and offline religious observance: "The survey suggests that religious engagement through TV, radio, music and the internet generally complements–rather than replaces–traditional kinds of religious participation, such as going to church." [13]

With older Catholics likelier to be in church than online, and with young adults likelier to be online than in church, digital evangelization becomes an essential first step to address an even broader generational challenge. Analyzing the National Study of Youth and Religion (NSYR) that surveyed more than 3,000 US Catholic millennials as they transitioned from ages 13 to 17 in 2002 into young adulthood at ages 18 to 23 in 2007,[14] sociologist Christian Smith noted the collapse of the intergenerational system whereby Catholics pass on the faith to their children. This system characterized the postwar period from 1945 to 1970, the formative decades of the Baby Boomers, a generation that rejected authority as well as many childhood beliefs and habits. In his 2014 NSYR analysis, co-written with three colleagues, Smith observed that during these key Vatican II transition years "no alternative approach to effective intergenerational Catholic faith transmission had been devised and instituted to replace the old system—and in-

---

13. Pew Research Center, Nov. 6, 2014, "Religion and Electronic Media: One-in-Five Americans Share Their Faith Online."

14. Although the US Catholic bishops have traditionally identified people aged 18 to 39 as "young adults," Smith's summary of data on "young Catholics" actually limits itself to "emerging adults" aged 18 to 23.

deed it is not clear that any such effective system has yet been put in place even today."[15]

Although many Boomers have followed a statistical pattern of returning to their faith later in life, the NSYR study confirmed that their parental influence over children diminishes after the latter leave home; Smith observes that whether, as emerging adults, Catholic millennials continue to attend Mass or pray "depends to a large extent" on whether they experienced a strong Catholic culture in their families as teens. Emerging adults in the study practiced their faith at ages 18 to 23 only if parents modeled it seriously (through relationships, practice, and identity) during those crucial adolescent years.[16] Where parents did not provide a strong Catholic culture for millennial teenagers, discussing and sharing the stories of their faith authentically, those children left home with little likelihood of ever returning to religion later in life.

The statistics offer no support for a strategy of waiting passively for them to come back. Whereas Boomers and even Generation X Catholics followed a cycle of disappearing from church after confirmation, then returning when they settled down, among millennials that rotation has broken down as marriage rates have declined in their age group. In a 2017 book-length study of US parishes, Georgetown University's Center for Applied Research in the Apostolate (CARA) said no evidence existed even at that time that millennials would one day return to religious participation of their own accord: "A key question not answered by these data is to what extent the millennials, a larger proportion of whom have been identi-

---

15. Christian Smith, Kyle Longest, Jonathan Hill, and Kari Christoffersen, *Young Catholic America: Emerging Adults In, Out of, and Gone from the Church* (Oxford: Oxford University Press, 2014), 26.
16. Smith, Longest, Hill, and Christoffersen, 66.

fying as nonreligious than previous generations . . . will follow the path of previous generations and become more active in their parishes as they age, get married, and have children."[17]

Millennials have proven almost as unlikely to encounter Catholicism online as to show up at a parish. From the earliest years after Facebook launched in 2004 and Apple released its first iPhone in 2007, Catholics have struggled to establish an attractive digital presence, particularly on the social networks millennials use. In a September 2012 new media survey of 1,047 self-identified Catholics aged 18 or older, commissioned by the United States Conference of Catholic Bishops (USCCB), CARA found that 53 percent of respondents said they were "unaware of any significant presence of the Catholic Church online." Another 11 percent said it was "not very visible," 12 percent said it was "only a little visible," 16 percent said it was "somewhat visible," and eight percent said it was "very visible."

While 23 percent of Catholics in this survey reported viewing religious or spiritual content on television, only 8 percent reported viewing religious or spiritual video content online (e.g., YouTube). Just 6 percent said they read content from a religious or spiritual website or blog, 3 percent read a religious or spiritual magazine or newspaper online, 2 percent read a religious or spiritual e-book (e.g., for Kindle, Nook), 4 percent listened to religious or spiritual programs on a mobile device or online, and one percent followed religious or spirituality related tweets on Twitter. The survey also noted Google

---

17. Charles Zech, Mary L. Gautier, Mark M. Gray, Jonathon L. Wiggins, and Thomas P. Gaunt, SJ, *Catholic Parishes of the 21st Century* (New York, Oxford University Press, 2017), 96.

Trends showing a declining occurrence of the word "Catholic" in broader religious content search volumes.

Despite their popularity with niche audiences, young adult Catholic blogs and webzines aimed at this generation—including Busted Halo, founded by the Paulist Fathers in 2000, and The Jesuit Post (now a platform of *America*) founded by Jesuit seminarians in 2012 around the time of the CARA study—evidently did not impact these survey results. That becomes an issue when considering how millennials go online as their primary source of information about the world. Compared to 38 percent of respondents overall who preferred online content in this study, a majority of millennials (52 percent) preferred it, reporting lack of interest as the primary reason they did not engage Catholic media online. Noting the need for Catholic digital outreach to cast a broader net, CARA concluded: "The challenge for the Church in this second decade of the twenty-first century is to reach more Catholics outside of this core which is more often populated by infrequent Mass attenders and a sizeable number of Millennials who use technology and new media but who say they are not interested enough in Catholic content to seek it out."[18]

Fortunately, when Catholic Christians model their faith with authenticity and a spirit of invitation, it remains as deeply attractive to people of all ages as in the time of Jesus and his first disciples. This online faith-sharing project will show that when believers share their religious experiences in a Facebook-based retreat with a focus on relationship, inviting people of all ages into spiritual conversations on the digital turf of young adults, people respond. Like many successful

---

18. Center for Applied Research in the Apostolate, November 2012, "Catholic New Media Use in the United States, 2012," 6.

evangelicals and followers of other religions, Catholics must simply want to be in relationship badly enough to talk about it; then they must master the participatory style of social media communication to interact a way that interests young people.

However much US Catholics have used the internet and social media, including more recent standouts like Bishop Robert Barron's laudable efforts to engage people in direct dialogues via his videos and podcasts at Word on Fire Ministries, few have used it successfully to reach beyond their generational bubbles. My Facebook group, building on the good start of the digital efforts just named, sought to offer Catholic media consumers a way to engage in a higher-participation style of faith-sharing than even these initiatives have provided. Far from considering his own videos and public dialogues the apotheosis of digital ministry, Barron himself points to this need to develop more participatory online faith dialogues: "From fairly extensive experience on Facebook and other social media websites, I know that people are adept when it comes to shouting about religion, but that very few know how to constructively, rationally, and helpfully enter into conversation about religious matters."[19]

To converse effectively about religious faith, as Barron suggests, believers must embrace an open mindset about sharing the stories of their prayer and religious experiences. The above statistics on the participatory shift of the digital revolution and the intergenerational disconnect it creates for Catholics all point to inclusivity as a key pastoral ingredient to make online evangelization more engaging. Millennials need pastoral accompaniment and sensitivity. Countering a pre-dig-

---

19. Robert Barron, *Arguing Religion: A Bishop Speaks at Facebook and Google* (Park Ridge, IL: Word on Fire, 2018), iv.

ital mindset that favors marketing prepackaged catechetical programming and waiting for millennials to find it, Jared Dees notes: "For young-adult ministry, though, people have to be convinced to join. They will not have any motivation to come on their own. They will have to be invited."[20]

The Story of Millennials

Building on this conviction that Catholics must reach out to young people on the margins of religion, Pope Francis has challenged believers to hear God's call "to go forth from our own comfort zone in order to reach all the 'peripheries' in need of the light of the Gospel."[21] To answer this call with millennials, people of faith must listen to their distinctive pastoral needs. While believers might want to reach disaffiliated young people, and even to do so using new media, studies infer it will be progressively more difficult because "the already-large share of religiously unaffiliated millennial adults is increasing significantly" over time as this generation drives the growth of the "nones" across all age groups.[22] The Covid-19 shutdown of churches deepened this trend, with only 25 percent of 2,214 self-identified US Catholics from ages 18 to 35 (covering most millennials and some older iGeneration Catholics) reporting to CARA in July and August 2020 that they participated in a

---

20. Jared Dees, *To Heal, Proclaim, and Teach: The Essential Guide to Ministry in Today's Catholic Church* (Notre Dame: Ave Maria Press, 2016), 265.

21. Pope Francis, Apostolic Exhortation *Evangelii Gaudium* [The Joy of the Gospel], Nov. 24, 2013, no. 20, Holy See, https://w2.vatican.va/content/francesco/en/apost_exhortations/documents/papa-francesco_esortazione-ap_20131124_evangelii-gaudium.html.

22. Michael Lipka, "Millennials Increasingly Are Driving Growth of 'Nones,'" Pew Research Center (May 12, 2015), https://www.pewresearch.org/fact-tank/2015/05/12/millennials-increasingly-are-driving-growth-of-nones/.

televised or online Mass "somewhat" or "very often" during summer quarantine, and a full 36 percent of young respondents planning to attend Mass less often when parishes reopened.[23] Far from simply posting videos of religious events like Mass, a special kind of outreach will be needed with young people, one of an enhanced inclusivity involving highly participatory media that accompanies them in their concerns.

As I write these words, "young adults" and "millennials" remain largely equivalent terms. While some members of the iGeneration (Generation Z, born 1997-2012) had entered legal adulthood by the time of my Facebook faith-sharing retreat in October 2020, the respondents aged 18-29 that Pew reported likeliest to engage online faith-sharing in 2014 all came from Generation Y, the millennials, and most existing research on "young Christians" still covered just this generation. Pew fixes Generation Y birth years at 1981-1996 for "key political, economic and social factors," including the 9/11 terror attacks.[24] At these ages, placing them between college graduation and age 39 during the time of my retreat, digitally literate millennials comprise the majority of young married couples and potential Rite of Christian Initiation of Adults (RCIA) candidates that US Catholic parishes need most badly. They also face stronger obstacles than any prior generation to sitting down in the pews, manifesting a trend that research suggests will intensify in the iGeneration coming after them.

23. Mark M. Gray, "New Poll: 36 Percent of Young Catholics Say They Will Attend Mass Less Often After Pandemic," *America: The Jesuit Review* (Sept. 14, 2020), https://www.americamagazine.org/faith/2020/09/14/poll-catholics-attend-mass-less-often-covid-19.

24. Michael Dimock, "Defining Generations: Where Millennials End and Post-Millennials Begin," *Fact Tank: News in the Numbers* (March 1, 2018), http://www.pewresearch.org/fact-tank/2018/03/01/defining-generations-where-millennials-end-and-post-millennials-begin/.

Research suggests that only a firm decision by believers to use social media, and to use it in an authentic way that makes young people feel invited and included in their faith communities, will change this trend. To master the highly participative interaction that attracts millennials in conversations both offline and online, it helps to start with the *via negativa* of what they do not like about the more packaged forms of community they find in institutional religion. Pro Church Tools, a free design resources hub for Christian congregations, gives five research-based reasons millennials do not attend church: Millennials find the church fake, exclusive, uncaring, aggressive/hyper-critical, and ignorant of issues relevant to their lives.[25]

More specific to Roman Catholicism, a 2017 collaborative study of disaffiliated young Catholics by Saint Mary's Press and CARA breaks them into the categories of drifters, injured, and dissenters who leave the Church because of six distinct dynamics: some precipitating event or events; cultural secularization; a sense of freedom in leaving; a desire to make religion a choice rather than something forced on them from above; a desire to be ethical without religion; and a need for rational proof to justify the parts they do not believe. Confirming Smith's emphasis on adolescence as a key period, this study identified 13 as the median age for millennials leaving the faith in 2013, and argued that initiating deeper conversations about faith would be the only way to address this trend. It concluded that the only way for Catholics to "articulate a compelling and convincing rationale for why religious affili-

---

25. Brady Shearer, "5 Research-Backed Reasons Millennials Are Done With Church," *Pro Church Tools* (Aug. 16, 2017), https://prochurchtools.com/millennials-stop-attending-church/.

ation and practice matters," especially to the growing number of families on the margins of Catholic parish life, would be to make their "primary pastoral motivation and action . . . to accompany young people on their spiritual journey" in an ongoing relationship that engages their questions and doubts.[26]

Other studies show that millennials respond well when they feel accompanied this way, so long as there's some informality to make them feel comfortable about opening up. An MTV "No Collar Workers" survey reported that in their quest for work-life balance, 89 percent of millennials want "to be constantly learning on the job" and 79 percent "want to be able to wear jeans to work sometimes."[27] For a generation that wants to engage deep issues in non-institutional settings, online interaction offers an ideal starting place to share the story of faith.

Although no study yet exists proving that millennials will start attending church after interacting online with a religious community in this way, the data suggest believers have much to gain by making a more determined effort. The one guaranteed way to not have millennials at church will be to do little or nothing online. More than any prior generation, millennials have shown a tendency to socialize offline with people they encounter online through dating websites like CatholicMatch.com or eHarmony.com (where many have met spouses) and through the "meetup group" phenomenon of young adults discussing common interests on social media

---

26. Robert J. McCarty and John M. Vitek, *Going, Going, Gone: The Dynamics of Disaffiliation in Young Catholics* (Winona, MN: Saint Mary's Press, 2017), 34.

27. David Mielach, "Gen Y Seeks Work-Life Balance Above All Else," *Business News Daily* (March 30, 2012), https://www.businessnewsdaily.com/2278-generational-employee-differences.html.

to organize offline gatherings, giving further reason to hope their online habits will impact offline practices when it comes to religion as well.[28]

Although the rise of agnosticism and atheism has driven the growth of the "nones," online evangelizers will also do well to appreciate that religiously unaffiliated millennials tend to be differently religious rather than areligious, maintaining some belief in a higher power and in spiritual practices like prayer. Noting how the period of emerging adulthood between self-identified child and self-identified adult has lengthened for millennials, who have not followed traditional benchmarks of maturity (i.e., graduation, career, marriage, children, financial independence) due to sociological changes propelling them through years of uncommitted wandering, Smith likewise prefers to think of the "nones" not as immature, but as differently mature, rejecting the popular phrase "extended adolescence" as imprecise due to their not being under the authority of educational institutions which regulate real adolescents.[29] When different generations mix in a social media setting like my Facebook group, more mature believers will do well to appreciate that the world has changed rapidly in recent decades, requiring of them a non-judgmental sensitivity toward millennials.

One key generational difference is that millennials grew up with more influence from the internet than from traditional educational sources like classrooms and libraries. That leads

---

28. One internet search for "meetup groups" in the St. Louis area revealed bagels, yoga, dancing lessons, swim lessons, and philosophy discussions available in summer 2020 even amid the Covid-19 quarantine.

29. Even though the NSYR focused on ages 18 to 23, no consensus yet exists on the age range of emerging adulthood, defined as the period when young people consider themselves neither children nor full adults.

them to filter the people and content they encounter to receive what makes them feel part of a group and to resist what seems like argumentative individualism. Sister Patricia Wittberg, SC, an American sociologist, observes that social media now pushes people of all ages toward the "social desirability bias" of consuming only what confirms the generational opinions and mindset they formed at age 20 to get along with peers and avoid fights. "We disproportionately pay attention to information that supports our point of view and resist information that disconfirms it," Wittberg writes, adding that Facebook links from friends and context-free Tweets make it "less likely that we will even *hear* viewpoints which differ from our own."[30]

Precisely because many millennials continue to believe in a higher power and pray even after severing congregational ties, they maintain some level of positive receptivity toward the authenticity of Christians who pray rather than just talk about prayer, who act on their beliefs by talking to God and to them in a participatory way. That emphasis on experiencing and sharing the story of faith, rather than simply exchanging information in a self-aggrandizing way, typifies the *Spiritual Exercises* that my retreat group followed. The US Catholic bishops have likewise insisted that praying sincerely rather than in a perfunctory way—even in the planning phase of evangelization—remains a particularly effective tool: "A planning process is permeated with prayer before, during, and after the process. Prayer is the most important work that the planning team will engage in. This is often an afterthought in

---

30. Patricia Wittberg, SC, *Catholic Cultures: How Parishes Can Respond to the Changing Face of Catholicism* (Collegeville: Liturgical Press, 2016), 56.

pastoral planning but must be kept at the forefront of pastoral planning efforts."[31]

A spirit of hospitality must ultimately permeate this prayerful spirit of invitation, accompaniment, and engagement in any successful faith-based outreach to millennials. Observing how Catholic communities move "from maintenance to mission" only when they include outsiders as welcome friends, the Paulist priest Robert Rivers writes: "Hospitality is what we extend to invited guests: family, friends, and business associates."[32]

The Story of Social Media

So how can believers use the youth-oriented platforms of social media for a dialogue that invites and unites people, rather than isolates and divides them? Many religious institutions employ a paid webmaster or public relations liaison to run social media accounts. It's not enough. The digital shift from packaged to participatory communication calls all believers to listen and speak from a more personal place, transcending any lingering notion of religion as solely a privatized devotion or channel of individual salvation to embrace a greater sense of communal responsibility for sharing the faith. By mixing generations in a faith-sharing retreat, my group sought to promote just that, demonstrating that a skillful use of media on Facebook can nourish people's desire for deeper connections with God and each other.

---

31. United States Conference of Catholic Bishops, *Living as Missionary Disciples: A Resource for Evangelization* (Washington, DC: United States Conference of Catholic Bishops, 2017), 20.

32. Robert S. Rivers, CSP, *From Maintenance to Mission: Evangelization and the Revitalization of the Parish* (New York: Paulist Press, 2005), 121.

Facebook, still the world's leading social network, provided the most fertile platform for mixing generations in my online faith-sharing retreat group. In CARA's 2012 new media survey, 62 percent of Catholics representing an estimated 36.2 million US adults reported having a Facebook profile in 2012, with 82 percent of millennials using Facebook as the highest percentage of any generation.[33] Overall, far more adult Catholics reported using Facebook than LinkedIn (17 percent), Google+ (15 percent), Twitter (13 percent), Pinterest (7 percent), Instagram (5 percent), Tumblr (1 percent), and other (1 percent) social media networks. Yet only four percent of Catholics from all generations reported visiting a Facebook account associated with Catholics or Catholic institutions. Considering that millennials reported spending three hours and forty-three minutes online during an average day, the most of any generation surveyed, these numbers confirm that all believers (and not only Catholics) have a lot to gain from an enhanced outreach on Facebook in particular.[34]

Secular research shows that people who connect online through Facebook or another platform become likelier to connect socially offline. Synthesizing data from her own work and other surveys, digital media researcher Nancy Baym reported in 2015 that "media use and face-to-face communication were positively correlated" and that internet users proved "generally more social than non-users" in being likelier to have a

---

33. While Facebook remains the most-used social media among all generations born before 1997, making it the ideal intergenerational meeting place to attract millennials for my retreat group, Snapchat passed it for first place among teenagers in 2016, making it likely that the iGeneration (aged eight to 24 at the time of this writing) will require different forms of digital evangelization when they come of age. For millennials, Instagram has become the second-most used social media site after Facebook.

34. CARA, "Catholic New Media Use in the United States, 2012," 5.

non-kin confidant as well as to visit friends and family in person.[35] Baym, who moved from academic life at the University of Kansas to work as Principal Researcher at Microsoft Research, adds hard data here to the anecdotal evidence that the way online habits influence offline behavior patterns provides lucrative data for digital advertising and business practices. Applying her findings to the Catholic Church, I hoped to see the same trend happening in the influence of my Facebook faith-sharing retreat group on offline and online habits, an area that I will say more about in later chapters.

Baym's findings add nuance to the books and articles of researcher Jean Twenge, whose cautions about the impact of internet use on children portray the emerging iGeneration (Generation Z) as "lonely, dislocated" youths sitting alone in their bedrooms for days on end,[36] relating to friends they only know online at the expense of offline relationships.[37] They likewise verify the anecdotal reports of US parents that their children talk online largely with friends they have already met at school, or peers they know through mutual friends, and rarely if ever with total strangers. Viewed together as complementary lenses, these findings of Baym and Twenge imply that those Christians who use digital technology conversationally will reach out more effectively to these isolated youths and be more engaged socially as faith communities in

---

35. Nancy Baym, *Personal Connections in the Digital Age* (Cambridge: Polity Press, 2015), 166.

36. Jean M. Twenge, "Have Smartphones Destroyed a Generation?" *The Atlantic* (September 2017), https://www.theatlantic.com/magazine/archive/2017/09/has-the-smartphone-destroyed-a-generation/534198/.

37. Pew defines the iGeneration, Generation Z, as beginning with people born in 1997. While some US media outlets like Bloomberg end the generation with people born in 2012, there remains no consensus about when this generation ends, and most of it has yet to enter the US workforce.

the twenty-first century than those who do not try.[38] To that
end, a more recent survey suggested online discussion groups
like this project's Facebook retreat could offer a valuable life-
line into supportive religious communities for maturing iG-
eneration youths who at ages 13 to 23 took solace in faith but
experienced "heightened levels of loneliness and isolation as
a result of social distancing" during March 2020 coronavirus
lockdowns, leading the US bishops to call for greater pastoral
accompaniment online.[39]

To borrow a word from the secular communications expert Brittany Hennessy, believers will do well not to dismiss
the impact of social networks on these isolated and lonely
young people, but to internalize the insight that all digital media users become potential "influencers" in a way that helps
young people feel a sense of social importance and agency. To
engage them in this active way requires basic digital literacy.
If evangelizers have not done so already, Hennessy hints that
a first step in learning how to use Facebook for faith-based
conversation will be to find a non-religious group that interests them and start participating: "There are so many Facebook groups for influencers categorized by location, vertical
(fashion, beauty, style, parenthood, food, DIY, etc.), and just
general interest. Join them, introduce yourself, ask people to
follow you, and ask for feedback on your content."[40]

---

38. Presuming, as my retreat group did in observance of safe environment
boundaries, that said young people are legal adults at least 18 years of age
or participating in a Catholic school program with appropriate supervision.
39. Christopher White, "Study Finds Young Strong in Faith Amid Virus, But
Increasingly Lonely," *Crux* (April 20, 2020), https://cruxnow.com/church-
in-the-usa/2020/04/study-finds-youth-strong-in-faith-amid-virus-but-in-
creasingly-lonely/.
40. Brittany Hennessy, *Influencer: Building Your Personal Brand in the Age of
Social Media* (New York: Citadel Press, 2018), 53.

The keys here will be authenticity and freedom of expression, not staged presentation. Whether Facebook users join Bishop Barron's Word on Fire community to watch his video commentaries on popular culture and dialogues with non-believers, or join an *America* discussion group, social media experts suggest viewing Facebook as a digital extension of existing personalities and relationships, an opportunity for spontaneous expression. Keith Anderson, a Lutheran pastor from Generation X, coined the phrase "digital cathedral" to describe the online presence of Christian communities. He sees social networks like Facebook as chances for Christians to "sacralize" the digital space by sharing our faith on it. Anderson challenges Christians to reimagine smart phones as places, not things, and to envision social networks as extensions of local faith communities which can feel as real to young adults as offline encounters felt to previous generations: "Although the digital networks like Facebook and Twitter are relatively new, networks themselves are not. They have always existed, whether we recognized or could name them as such."[41]

Reframing Facebook as a place for ministry, Anderson's work supported my decision to adapt the traditional practice of a moderated faith-sharing group to a digital retreat rather than simply post videos or monitor an unmoderated topical discussion forum. In "Click2Save Reboot," Anderson and Catholic religious studies scholar Elizabeth Drescher of Santa Clara University present Christian participation in social media prayer events and digital worship as more than just a way to deliver canned information about offline activities. When Christian pastors strategically engage "digitally enabled re-

---

41. Keith Anderson, *The Digital Cathedral: Networked Ministry in a Wireless World* (New York: Morehouse Publishing, 2015), 51.

lationships," responding to what Drescher calls the "Digital Reformation," online events strengthen people's ties to God and to the community. Anderson and Drescher write: "Multiply that by the healthy percentage of mainline Protestants and Catholics among the more than two billon Facebook users, and you get a sense of the impact of social media on the church and on Christian ministry today."[42] Facebook's broad demographic reach also makes it ideal for digital outreach. At the time of my retreat group, Facebook remained the social network where millennials and earlier generations crossed paths most often. In a guidebook for parish digital outreach, Archdiocese of Boston media strategist Scot Landry cited statistics that 166 million Americans already used Facebook in 2014, more than half (52.9 percent) of the overall population at the time. In response, Landry encouraged regular churchgoers to share faith-based photos, homily videos, and links online in a personalized way. He also asked parishes to train laypeople to participate directly on faith-based social media channels, making Catholic Facebook pages into spaces where all people (not just paid staff or volunteers) participate informally in a fun way: "For those not yet on Facebook but on the Internet, the parish can help them connect with friends, relatives, kids, and grandkids by training them on Facebook and then encouraging them to tithe 10 percent or more of their social media messages or likes to faith-related content. The parish can also encourage parishioners to connect with one another on Facebook, not just with their friends from youth sports, universities, high schools, and the like."[43]

---

42. Keith Anderson and Elizabeth Drescher, *Click2Save Reboot: The Digital Ministry Bible* (New York: Church Publishing, 2018), 3.

43. Scot Landry, *Transforming Parish Communications: Growing the Church Through New Media* (Huntington, IN: Our Sunday Visitor, 2014), 116.

Essentially an online bulletin board that allows people to respond to each other in real time with a variety of audio-visual tools like live-stream videos with comment discussion threads, Facebook reaches across time zones by allowing asynchronous participation in a private group, making it more flexible than videoconferencing platforms like Zoom or Skype which require people to be in one place at the same time with a perfect internet connection. That flexibility offers both benefits and limitations, leading secular technology blogger Heather Mansfield to admonish non-profits in a 2012 book to stay humble in their expectations when using the platform: "Although Facebook has helped fuel revolutions (literally), this was not done through the use of the Facebook Page tool set. It was the people themselves, organizing and communicating with their friends and family on Facebook, who did it." [44] In other words, *who* uses Facebook and *how* they use it remain more determinative of its influence than the platform in and of itself, as the key ingredient for success remains the relational attitude people bring to it.

Reflecting McLuhan's insight that the quality of interaction determines the depth of a medium's influence, Facebook has wisely fine-tuned its mix of personal and branded content to avoid being swamped by advertisers pushing prepackaged materials. Effective Facebook communication still seeks to connect rather than privatize people, and British social media consultant Andrew Macarthy praises the platform's efforts to achieve this balance: "It makes sense, given that Facebook users primarily visit the site to interact with their friends and family and they want to see their posts, but they *also* visit

---

44. Heather Mansfield, *Social Media for Social Good: A How-To Guide for Nonprofits* (New York: McGraw-Hill, 2012), 88.

Facebook to be informed, inspired, to converse with likeminded people, and be entertained—which is where you come in."[45]

These secular best practices encourage believers to personalize Facebook interactions, dialoguing with people as fellow seekers. A personal touch fosters positive experiences of closeness in any online group. My retreat likewise showcased the value of a Facebook group that I intentionally set up with a mix of branded content (the *Exercises)* and personal availability (myself, a longtime Jesuit, as facilitator) in a context of overt faith-sharing, a venture that turned out to be both possible and demonstrably helpful to increasing people's sense of spiritual connection with God, self, and others.

Conclusion: Shifting Catholic Attitudes

Illustrating the story of new media from a Catholic perspective, in his 2019 post-synodal apostolic exhortation to young people Pope Francis quoted a lengthy comment from the bishops' final document. It is worth citing as a frame for sharing the faith online:

> The web and social networks have created a new way to communicate and bond. They are "a public square where the young spend much of their time and meet one another easily, even though not all have equal access to it, particularly in some regions of the world. They provide an extraordinary opportunity for dialogue, encounter and exchange between persons, as well as access to information and knowledge. Moreover, the digital world is one of social and political engagement and active citizen-

---

45. Andrew Macarthy, *500 Social Media Marketing Tips: Essential Advice, Hints and Strategy for Business* (Self-Published, 2018), 44.

ship, and it can facilitate the circulation of independent information providing effective protection for the most vulnerable and publicizing violations of their rights. In many countries, the internet and social networks already represent a firmly established forum for reaching and involving young people, not least in pastoral initiatives and activities." Yet to understand this phenomenon as a whole, we need to realize that, like every human reality, it has its share of limitations and deficiencies . . . . Indeed, "the digital environment is also one of loneliness, manipulation, exploitation and violence, even to the extreme case of the 'dark web.' Digital media can expose people to the risk of addiction, isolation and gradual loss of contact with concrete reality, blocking the development of authentic interpersonal relationships."[46]

Behold the blessing and the curse of digital media, its ability to unite or to alienate, depending on our participatory skillfulness. Like all media, digital media can be used well (for dialogue, encounter, exchange, and engagement) or poorly. Later in this exhortation, Francis notes how the digital shift in media calls believers to embrace a parallel shift in evangelization:

> Youth ministry, as traditionally carried out, has been significantly affected by social and cultural changes. Young people frequently fail to find in our usual programmes a response to their concerns, their needs, their problems and issues. The proliferation and growth of

---

46. Francis, Post-Synodal Apostolic Exhortation *Christus Vivit* [Christ is Alive], March 25, 2019, no. 87, Holy See, http://w2.vatican.va/content/francesco/en/apost_exhortations/documents/papa-francesco_esortazione-ap_20190325_christus-vivit.html.

groups and movements predominantly associated with the young can be considered the work of the Holy Spirit who constantly shows us new paths. Even so, there is a need to look at the ways such groups participate in the Church's overall pastoral care, as well as a need for greater communion among them and a better coordination of their activities. Although it is never easy to approach young people, two things have become increasingly evident: the realization that the entire community has to be involved in evangelizing them, and the urgent requirement that young people take on a greater role in pastoral outreach.[47]

To make millennials feel welcome, Francis affirms McLuhan's insight that media outreach must engage them as active agents, not passive recipients. Here he grasps the truth that young people want not only to be seen, but to be heard and understood in a way that fosters communion rather than division. Summarizing again the bishops' final report in the synod on youth, Francis identifies what young people can teach pastors about shifting from packaged to participatory media: "The young make us see the need for new styles and new strategies. For example, while adults often worry about having everything properly planned, with regular meetings and fixed times, most young people today have little interest in this kind of pastoral approach. Youth ministry needs to become more flexible: inviting young people to events or occasions that provide an opportunity not only for learning, but also for conversing, celebrating, singing, listening to real stories and experiencing a shared encounter with the living God."[48]

---

47. Francis, Post-Synodal Apostolic Exhortation *Christus Vivit*, no. 202.
48. Francis, Post-Synodal Apostolic Exhortation *Christus Vivit*, no. 204.

The phrase "not only for learning, but also for conversing" affirms my choice to use faith-sharing as my retreat group's primary mode of outreach to the frontiers of social media. The digital revolution has created a participatory culture with anti-hierarchical structures (not without their own inequalities, despite the apparent democracy of social networking culture) in online conversations. To move effectively beyond the "packaging devices" of McLuhan's terminology into a high participation outreach to emerging adults, Catholics must likewise shift our theology of communications—not merely our technology—in a way that embraces social media as a new ecclesial structure or expression of religious community.

Supporting this mental leap of insight that Francis sees social media demanding of Catholics, one seminal study defines the participatory culture of digital media as follows:

> As a set of ideals, we can define participatory culture in opposition to various forms of culture that limit access to the means of cultural production and circulation, that fragment and isolate the public rather than providing opportunities to create and share culture, and that construct hierarchies that make it difficult for many to exert any meaningful influence over the core decisions that impact their lives. People participate through and within communities: participatory culture requires us to move beyond a focus on individualized personal expression; it is about an ethos of "doing it together" in addition to "doing it yourself."[49]

---

49. Henry Jenkins, Mizuko Ito, and Dana Boyd, *Participatory Culture in a Networked Era* (Cambridge: Polity Press, 2018), 181.

Therein arises a paradox for a highly structured faith community like the Catholic Church: Even as this "participatory culture" of social media frustrates all hierarchical efforts of thought leaders (e.g., bishops, politicians, and the so-called mainstream media of the journalism establishment) to control people's perceptions through prepackaged manipulations of sound and image, it offers a more dynamic way to unite people in community as Francis hopes, rather than fragmenting them further into the intergenerational and interpersonal silos that low-participation media feeds. Like earlier forms of new media, digital technology has shifted relational patterns in a way that may strengthen the global Catholic Church, but only if Catholics work together rather than alone.

That will require older generations of religious believers, steeped in a more passive catechetical and media culture from childhood, to become comfortable with sharing their faith stories online. Web researcher John Dyer noted in 2011 that when he asked Christians "Is online community *real* community," millennials and others born after 1981 tended to answer "yes" while those of earlier generations said "online" and "community" did not "even make sense in the same sentence." Since "the function of social media is to connect physically distant people," Dyer concludes: "Our question then should not be 'Is it *real*?' because connecting online is just as 'real' as talking on the phone or sending a letter. The better question is, what are the rules of the medium and what are the underlying messages and patterns that emerge from these rules?"[50]

Dyer, who works at Dallas Theological Seminary, talks in detail from a Protestant perspective about how God himself

---

50. John Dyer, *From the Garden to the City: The Redeeming and Corrupting Power of Technology* (Grand Rapids: Kregel Publications, 2011), 167.

43

(in the Ten Commandments, for instance) and Christians have used new media to share faith. Social media represents only the latest technology in a two thousand-year Christian tradition of media appropriations that have sought to engage young people, build up faith communities, and help evangelizers witness publicly to their faith. Chapter 2 will review magisterial literature on mass communications to tell the story of how the Catholic Church since Vatican II offers three theological foundations for the faith-based use of new media: *communio,* synodality, and New Evangelization. Chapter 3 will tell the story of the participants in my online faith-sharing retreat group, chapter 4 will deepen that story in looking at their responses to pre-retreat and post-retreat surveys, and chapter 5 will offer a handbook for digital outreach that includes tentative conclusions based on my group's experience and ten research-based recommendations for future efforts to share the faith online.

From Packaged
to Participatory Church

This second chapter tells the story of the parallel shift from a packaged to a participatory church, reviewing magisterial literature on mass media since Vatican II to outline a papal theology of communications. It presents *communio,* synodality, and the New Evangelization as theological foundations of these teachings drawn from the Catholic tradition to inform the efforts of my project to create a more participatory digital extension of Catholic community in a Facebook faith-sharing group based on the Ignatian *Spiritual Exercises.* The world of social communications has changed significantly since the Second Vatican Council, with the rise of high-participation and low-information social media (distinct from what the media theorist McLuhan called non-participative, high-information, packaged media) bringing to spiritual conversations a new dynamism that calls out for faith-based adaptation. To use social media for digital evangelization, Catholics in particular need dialogue rather than monologue in all of their spiritual conversations, moving from formalized declamations (which tend shut down young people) into relationship-building. Theologically, the shift to participatory communication in digital media parallels the post-conciliar papacy's creative retrieval of apostolic *communio* as "the personal union of each human being with the divine Trinity and with the rest of mankind," leading to more participatory forms of synodality and New Evangelization.[51]

The Shift of *Communio*: Ecclesial Retrieval

Following a parallel shift in the way they communicate to a digital world, secular mass media and the Catholic Church have developed, according to McLuhan's terminology, from a one-way style of depersonalized information-delivery that binds relationships in fixed categories into a multi-directional interpersonal dialogue that reshapes relational hierarchies more fluidly. Just as the digital revolution of social media has flattened the authority of traditional journalists by placing them on an equal footing with amateurs posting viral videos of news events online, it has diluted the hierarchal authority of various churches, creating a global network of believers able to appropriate elements of faith for varied uses and converse instantaneously across vast distances. By developing the Vatican II emphasis on synodality, decentralizing magisterial authority to empower ground-level pastoral solutions particularly with family and youth issues, Francis has advanced the efforts of his papal predecessors to retrieve apostolic *communio*, modeling for digital evangelizers a participatory communications style well-suited to social media initiatives like an online faith-sharing group.

The story of a participatory and networked media culture, although it may seem like an invention of the digital

---

51. Congregation for the Doctrine of the Faith, *Letter to the Bishops of the Catholic Church on Some Aspects of the Church Understood as Communion,* May 28, 1992, no. 3, http://www.vatican.va/roman_curia/congregations/cfaith/documents/rc_con_cfaith_doc_28051992_communionis-notio_en.html.

revolution with roots in McLuhan's 1960s writings, strongly evokes the ecclesial culture of early Christianity, where diverse faith communities spoke freely about their challenges to discern unified pastoral responses. In the Pauline epistles that dominate biblical records of the apostolic period, the paradox appears of a *patriarchal but not hierarchical Church* emerging gradually from its Jewish roots, scattered geographically but united by an open yet messy spirit of dialogue. Some key aspects of this early Christian ecclesiology of *communio,* the theological term that Vatican II and post-conciliar popes have retrieved, will help contextualize the digital revolution's influence on recent synodal developments under Francis.

Forming community through conversation, the early Christians creatively adapted their Jewish roots to the way they shared their faith in Jesus. Saul of Tarsus—that great Christian convert from Second Temple Judaism, with its caste of hereditary male priests offering cultic sacrifice—established a traditional patriarchal ecclesiology in communities he founded across Asia Minor. But he did so by traveling outside the Jewish clerical hierarchy to establish loose networks of house churches among Greek and Roman pagans, becoming the most innovative evangelizer of early Christianity, wisely using written media to counsel and lead them.[52] While he stayed tied to a Mediterranean cultural milieu that identified clergy with *patriarchs*, married family men who led houses of worship, the Christian emphasis on his pagan Greek name "Paul" signaled Saul's departure from hierarchies tied to the Mosaic Law. In his domestic churches, patriarchs like Paul reserved the right to make the final decisions, but allowed all

---

52. Of the twenty-seven books in the Greek New Testament, thirteen are epistles of St. Paul to his communities.

stakeholders of any social rank or background to give input on issues facing the community.

Theologically, this participatory ecclesiology reflected the idea of *communio,* the unity in diversity that Vatican II saw as a key lesson of early Christianity to help the Church relate more effectively to the modern world. Ladislas Orsy, a Hungarian canonist who advised the bishops at Vatican II and into his late 90s continued to promote the Council's spirit, defines *communio* as "the inner life of God, who is one God in three persons," modeling the "unity in diversity, or diversity in unity" that calls Christians to live as a family of many believers in one "house of God." Orsy writes: "The one Spirit of Christ dwells in many and holds them together. Briefly but substantially, this is the theological reality of *communio.* All external manifestations of unity, such as collegiality and solidarity, flow from it. Among human beings, composed of spirit and matter, the internal and invisible mystery needs to manifest itself externally and visibly. One cannot exist without the other, not in this universe where the Word has become flesh."[53]

For Orsy, this spirit of *communio* permeates the relationships of all participatory Christian communities since the apostolic age. Therefore, he asks: What external structures best express, promote, and sustain this internal bond of unity in diversity? Synodality has traditionally dominated Eastern Christian ecclesiology as the preferred response to that question, but Orsy laments that Western Christianity gradually neglected it due to the papacy's top-down policies. Having become centralized under the papacy, the Roman Catholic Church increasingly embraced a packaged communications

---

53. Ladislas Orsy, SJ, *Receiving the Council: Theological and Canonical Insights and Debates* (Collegeville: Michael Glazier, 2009), 5.

style of monologue over bottom-up synodal dialogue, privileging the one-way pronouncements of media like papal bulls. As synods grew less frequent in the West especially during the three centuries between the Council of Trent and the First Vatican Council, Roman Catholics came to forget this privileged apostolic expression of collegial solidarity, a profound act of *communio* first seen in the Council of Jerusalem's decision that Gentile converts needn't follow the Mosaic Law.[54]

Interestingly enough, from the very office that neglected it for so long, recent popes have gradually restored and developed Western synodality. This papal restoration of synodality began at the Second Vatican Council, itself a profound exercise of communion, with a call back to St. Paul's ecclesiology. In the documents of Vatican II, the idea of *communio* as inspiration for renewing ecclesial structures appears in multiple references to the Church as "the Body of Christ," an image from Paul's words to the community in Corinth:[55] "As a body is one though it has many parts, and all the parts of the body, though many, are one body, so also Christ."[56] Reflecting its own ecclesial witness of this Pauline unity in diversity as an assembly of episcopal collegiality modeled on the early Church, the Council refers to itself throughout its documents as "this Sacred Synod."[57]

Suggesting a theological model for how Catholics might interact on social media today, Paul expands on *communio* else-

---

54. See Acts 15:2-35.
55. Second Vatican Council, Dogmatic Constitution *Lumen gentium* [On the Church], Nov. 27, 1964, no. 8, http://www.vatican.va/archive/hist_councils/ii_vatican_council/documents/vat-ii_const_19641121_lumen-gentium_en.html.
56. 1 Cor. 12:12.
57. Second Vatican Council, *Lumen gentium*, no. 1.

where, emphasizing the humble collegiality Jesus embodies. Urging believers to base their unity in diversity on the triune communion of divine persons, Paul tells the Philippians: "If there is any encouragement in Christ, any solace in love, any participation in the Spirit, any compassion and mercy, complete my joy by being of the same mind, with the same love, united in heart, thinking one thing. Do nothing out of selfishness or out of vainglory; rather, humbly regard others as more important than yourselves, each looking out not for his own interests, but [also] everyone for those of others. Have among yourselves the same attitude that is also yours in Christ Jesus."[58]

Commenting on this passage, the American biblical theologian Robert F. O'Toole notes how Paul exhorts his community to think the same things in the Lord, with the imperative of fellowship (a sense of solidarity among equals) driving an authentic consensus about Christian unity that arises from genuine concern for the good of all in the group: "What interests us is the moral directive to the members of the community to think the same thing and the approval given to the various expressions of fellowship noted in the epistle."[59] If unity of thought and action remains supreme in the Christian moral life for Paul here, it still does not destroy the diversity of what O'Toole calls the Philippians' "various expressions of fellowship."

Theological images of *communio* in this chapter have thus far included collegiality, synodality, solidarity, the body of Christ, and fellowship, but a particularly apt one comes from Pope Benedict XVI. In a brief but influential 2009 address, Benedict XVI promoted a relational model of "co-re-

---

58. Phil. 2:1-5.
59. Robert F. O'Toole, SJ, *Who Is a Christian? A Study in Pauline Ethics* (Eugene: Wipf & Stock, 1990), 46.

sponsibility" between clergy and laity in Catholic communities, rooting ecclesial *communio* in the early Christian witness of fraternal charity that he will also insist upon as a model for internet exchanges: "Lastly, the witness of charity that unites hearts and opens them to ecclesial belonging should not be forgotten. Historians answer the question as to how the success of Christianity in the first centuries can be explained, the ascent of a presumed Jewish sect to the religion of the Empire, by saying that it was the experience of Christian charity in particular that convinced the world."[60]

Comparing this co-responsible charity of the early Christian communities to the more hierarchical structures they developed into, for good and for ill, the Australian Jesuit systematic theologian Gerald O'Collins concludes that the biblical witness creates an "issue of public credibility" challenging today's Catholic clergy to adopt a more collegial attitude toward others: "No amount of scriptural and theological argument about continuity in apostolic faith in Christ will prove successful apologetically, without the visible witness to that faith being embodied in the life and worship of those exercising the ordained ministry and the episcopal office."[61] Since Vatican II, popes from Paul VI to Francis have labored to foster this witness, using mass media in varied ways to help express *communio* through synods.

---

60. Benedict XVI, Address of His Holiness Pope Benedict XVI *Opening of the Pastoral Convention of the Diocese of Rome on the Theme: "Church Membership and Pastoral Co-Responsibility,"* May 26, 2009, Holy See, http://w2.vatican.va/content/benedict-xvi/en/speeches/2009/may/documents/hf_ben-xvi_spe_20090526_convegno-diocesi-rm.html.
61. Gerald O'Collins, SJ, *Rethinking Fundamental Theology: Toward a New Fundamental Theology* (Oxford: Oxford University Press, 2011), 290.

Synodality from Paul VI to Francis

At Vatican II, the Catholic Church's *ressourcement* (return to the sources of faith) unfolded paradoxically in the context of the *aggiornamento* (bringing up to date) that Pope John XXIII introduced to "throw open the windows" of the hierarchical Church to the modern world. To move forward in an age of mass media, the Church went backward, looking to early Christianity for guidance. Even before the Council authorized sweeping reforms to every aspect of Catholicism, observers felt fresh ecclesial winds blowing in the novelty of press, film, radio, and television covering an ecumenical council for the first time in history. It reflected a more inclusive way of communicating that softened the authoritarian style dominant since the counter-reformation polemics of the Council of Trent (1545-1563) and the definition of papal infallibility at the First Vatican Council (1869-1870) that confirmed the pope's authority over faith and morals in dogmatic definitions without requiring any recourse to episcopal consensus.

Thanks to this mass media coverage, Vatican II became the most transparent ecumenical council in history, inviting people across the globe to follow its conversations as participatory witnesses of unity in diversity. In its short Decree on the Media of Social Communications *(Inter Mirifica)* that Paul VI promulgated at the end of 1963, the Council endorsed the catechetical value of four media platforms, urging episcopal conferences to use them with moral responsibility to form people's consciences: "Since an effective apostolate on a national scale calls for unity of planning and resources, this sacred Synod decrees and orders that national offices for affairs of the press, films, radio and television be established everywhere and given every aid."[62] These four platforms (notably including McLuhan's participatory exemplar of television, where Archbishop Fulton J. Sheen had become an early televangelist)[63] enabled the Catholic hierarchy to deliver prepackaged catechesis in the sender-receiver style of a theater production or advertising piece, evangelizing people through canned programming that still went far beyond the reach of more traditional media. Near the Council's end, on September 15, 1965, Paul VI created the Synod of Bishops as a permanent advisory body to the pope, a tool of collaboration-at-papal-discretion (as distinct from collegial governance) that would soon use mass media for ecclesial consultations like the two *Humanae Vitae* commissions of 1968.

After Vatican II, Paul VI's annual World Communications Day addresses from 1967 to 1978 kept highlighting these four platforms as instruments of *communio*, and in documents like the 1971 Instruction on the Means of Social Communication *(Communio et Progressio)* he called for Catholics to acquire basic media literacy. Modeling that literacy, he favored a standard media blueprint for his synods (1967, 1969, 1971, 1974, and 1977) of bishops: The Vatican would consult global stakeholders on a topic; the bishops would gather for collaborative dialogue amplified in press, radio, television, and film;

---

62. Second Vatican Council, Decree *Inter Mirifica* [On Social Communications], Dec. 4, 1963, no. 13, http://www.vatican.va/archive/hist_councils/ ii_vatican_council/documents/vat-ii_decree_19631204_inter-mirifica_ en.html.

63. Archbishop Fulton J. Sheen, an early Catholic evangelizer on radio and television, hosted the inspirational television program *Life is Worth Living* on DuMont (1952-1955, during which it won the network's only Emmy) and later ABC (1955-1957) as well as two other series from 1958-1968. The original television show competed with Milton Berle as the top-rated US network television program of its day.

then the pope would issue a post-synodal apostolic exhortation for pastoral guidance to the Church. In *Evangelii Nuntiandi,* his 1975 exhortation on evangelization that John Paul II later cited as wellspring of the New Evangelization and that Francis credited as inspiration for *Evangelii Gaudium,* Paul VI affirmed an essential link between evangelization and mass media, building on Vatican II's reframing of the Church from an inward-looking fortress of declamatory monologue to an outward-looking gospel witness seeking faith-based dialogue with modernity: "Our century is characterized by the mass media or means of social communication, and the first proclamation, catechesis or the further deepening of faith cannot do without these means, as we have already emphasized."[64]

Subsequent popes built steadily upon this magisterial zeal for evangelizing through mass communications. Pope John Paul I did not live long enough to give a World Communications Day address. But Pope John Paul II took Paul VI's link between media and evangelization a step further, in a prophetic 1990 passage that asked to integrate the gospel message into the increasingly participatory culture of mass media itself: "There is a deeper reality involved here: since the very evangelization of modern culture depends to a great extent on the influence of the media, it is not enough to use the media simply to spread the Christian message and the Church's authentic teaching. It is also necessary to integrate that message into the 'new culture' created by modern communications."[65]

---

64. Paul VI, Post-Synodal Apostolic Exhortation *Evangelii Nuntiandi* [On Evangelization in the Modern World], Dec. 8, 1975, no. 45, http://w2. vatican.va/content/paul-vi/en/apost_exhortations/documents/hf_p-vi_ exh_19751208_evangelii-nuntiandi.html.

65. John Paul II, Encyclical Letter *Redemptoris Missio* [Mission of the Redeemer], Dec. 7, 1990, no. 37, http://w2.vatican.va/content/john-paul-ii/

Under John Paul II this transition to a more participatory Church remained limited due to the pre-digital culture of mass media. The Holy See began its website www.vatican.va under his long papacy, during which the Synod of Bishops assembled fifteen times. But when he died in 2005, the digital age with its less packaged media platforms had barely started. Moving ahead into the digital revolution, his successor Benedict XVI became the first pope to use a Twitter account and to discuss social media explicitly in his annual World Communications Day messages, further integrating evangelization into mass media culture.

In 2011, at a point relatively early in the digital revolution when Facebook was thriving and early-generation smartphones had appeared, Benedict focused his annual communications address on the need for Christians to bring authenticity to their faith witness on social networks: "It follows that there exists a Christian way of being present in the digital world: this takes the form of a communication which is honest and open, responsible and respectful of others. To proclaim the Gospel through the new media means not only to insert expressly religious content into different media platforms, but also to witness consistently, in one's own digital profile and in the way one communicates choices, preferences and judgements that are fully consistent with the Gospel, even when it is not spoken of specifically."[66]

---

en/apost_constitutions/documents/hf_jp-ii_apc_15081990_ex-corde-ecclesiae.html.

66. Benedict XVI, *Truth, Proclamation and Authenticity of Life in the Digital Age* [Message of His Holiness on the 45th World Communications Day], June 5, 2011, http://w2.vatican.va/content/benedict-xvi/en/messages/communications/documents/hf_ben-xvi_mes_20110124_45th-world-communications-day.html.

For Benedict XVI, the gospel witness of charitable *communio* remains central to any participatory Christian interaction on digital media. Ecclesiastically, he still relied on traditional media strategies in the assemblies he called of the Synod of Bishops, with the increasingly outdated Holy See Press Office operating on a news release and press conference model of one-way communication. But after Benedict resigned the papacy in 2013, the digital revolution intensified under his successor Francis, who in 2015 merged all the communications offices of Vatican City and the Holy See into the digitally minded Dicastery for Communication.[67]

Developing the magisterial teaching of Benedict on evangelizing through digital charity, Francis chose a *communio*-infused theme for World Communications Day 2019, consciously echoing a similar motif from his 2014 address that urged Christians to be examples of human solidarity online: 'We are members one of another' (Eph 4,25). From network community to human communities." In this 53rd World Day of Communications text, Francis returned to the body of Christ image from Vatican II as a synodal model for Christian digital relations, evoking McLuhan's participatory criteria of embodiment: "The image of the body and the members reminds us that the use of the *social web* is complementary to an encounter in the flesh that comes alive through the body, heart, eyes, gaze, breath of the other."[68]

---

67. This merger of the Pontifical Council for Social Communications, the Vatican website, Vatican News (including the former Vatican Television Center), the Holy See Press Office, *L'Osservatore Romano*, Photograph Service, Vatican Radio, Vatican Press, and the Vatican Publishing House updated papal media for a digital age.

68. Francis, "We Are Members One of Another (Eph 4:25): From Social Network Communities to the Human Community" [Message of His Holiness on the 53rd World Communications Day], Jan. 24, 2019, http://w2.vatican.

Like his predecessors, Francis strives to model *communio* in his use of mass media and synods, but with a more digitally fluid sense of participation. Keith Anderson, the Lutheran media analyst, says the "personal leadership stance" of Francis "lends itself to a social media world," and he praises the shift from packaged to participatory communication that manifested itself when Francis posed for a viral selfie with young admirers shortly after his election:

> Contrast Francis' selfie with the scene of Benedict XVI sending out the first papal tweet, sitting at a large desk, typing on the papal iPad, surrounded by cardinals and courtiers, captured by a staff photographer. Hey, that wasn't bad for an eighty-five-year-old pontiff. But it reveals something of Benedict's approach to social media, which resembled more broadcast media than social media, more one-to-many communication, rather than a many-to-many conversation—tweets as one-hundred-and-forty-character pronouncements from the pope, rather than a platform for relationality. Pope Francis expresses through his words, actions, and, yes, selfies, a desire to be in relationship, to be connected.[69]

This "desire to be in relationship, to be connected" even digitally belies the pope's status as a member of the Silent Generation born in 1936. Oriented by nature to conversation and community, Francis shares his faith in a way that pushes the papacy beyond repetition of past forms into a receptive encounter with new existential realities. At his opening ad-

---

va/content/francesco/en/messages/communications/documents/papa-francesco_20190124_messaggio-comunicazioni-sociali.html.

69. Keith Anderson, *The Digital Cathedral: Networked Ministry in a Wireless World* (New York: Morehouse Publishing, 2015), 63.

dresses for the two synods on the family, Francis sounded a participatory note in discussing the synodal process, as the American moral theologian Thomas Massaro observes:

> Francis used the Greek word *parrhesia*—meaning openness, frankness, even boldness—which captured his hopes for how the delegates would approach the proceedings. He encouraged the deliberations on the most sensitive issues regarding family life to proceed as a true dialogue, not as the tightly scripted monologues and ceremonial set pieces into which too many previous synods had devolved. No topic should be considered off the table; no one should be afraid to disagree with others, Francis advised. His sincere appeal to the delegates to speak their minds—sharing what was in their hearts rather than merely mouthing words they might suppose their peers or superiors would prefer to hear—changed the dynamics of the meeting in remarkable ways and by most accounts produced highly constructive results.[70]

The fact that Francis listened to people from all over the world in these meetings not only softened the distinction between clergy as "teaching church" and laity as "learning church" that reinforces a preference for monologue over dialogue, but also strengthened the synods' results. Rooted in participative discussions that included faith testimonies from married couples, the synods discerned creative pastoral ways to accompany families. They urged Catholics toward co-responsibility for implementing pastoral solutions at lower ecclesial levels, empowering dioceses and regions to craft

---

70. Thomas Massaro, SJ, *Mercy in Action: The Social Teachings of Pope Francis* (Lanham, Maryland: Rowman & Littlefield, 2018), 104.

pastoral plans in collaboration with Francis rather than wait passively for a Roman dicastery like the Congregation for the Doctrine of the Faith (CDF) to issue top-down decisions for them in packaged decrees.

In their interactions both offline and online, Francis wants all Catholics to practice this spirit of synodality, building unity through spiritual conversation. Defining it as "walking together," Francis chose synodality for the theme of the World Synod of Bishops now set to meet in October 2023, giving it this title: "For a synodal church: Communion, participation, and mission." By placing *communio*, collaborative discussion, and evangelization in the spotlight, this "synod on synodality" promises to develop a key idea of the pope's post-synodal apostolic exhortation on the family. Arguing for a collaborative diversity of pastoral interpretation within the unity of Catholic teaching, Francis writes in that document: "Since 'time is greater than space,' I would make it clear that not all discussions of doctrinal, moral or pastoral issues need to be settled by interventions of the magisterium. Unity of teaching and practice is certainly necessary in the Church, but this does not preclude various ways of interpreting some aspects of that teaching or drawing certain consequences from it."[71] Echoing the varied expressions of fellowship that O'Toole saw St. Paul approving in his letter to the Philippians, Francis draws from synodality the lesson that Catholics must recover a healthy respect for diverse perspectives in spiritual conversations if they wish to walk together in a truly communion-building way.

---

71. Francis, Post-Synodal Apostolic Exhortation *Amoris Laetitia* [The Joy of Love], no. 3, https://w2.vatican.va/content/dam/francesco/pdf/apost_exhortations/documents/papa-francesco_esortazione-ap_20160319_amoris-laetitia_en.pdf.

Applying the Catholic social justice principle of subsidiarity to the hierarchy itself, Francis insists on localized discussion before people ask the Vatican for input. By consulting widely at lower levels before making decisions, leadership consultant Chris Lowney sees Francis exporting the Ignatian governance of his religious order to the whole Catholic Church, adapting the *Constitutions of the Society of Jesus* that guided him especially as Jesuit provincial superior of Argentina from 1973 to 1979: "Both as provincial and as seminary head, Fr. Bergoglio was required to convene his 'consultors' regularly, a handful of Jesuit colleagues representing varying expertise, age groups, and points of view. When the system works well, decision quality invariably rises. Leaders must articulate their rationale, say, for wanting to launch a new ministry or replace a key lieutenant, and consultors can probe for blind spots or derailing 'attachments' that might be clouding the manager's judgment."[72]

When he created a Council of Cardinals in April 2013 as the papal equivalent of these Jesuit consultors, Francis insisted on hearing unfiltered clashing perspectives rather than just his own voice or the voices of flatterers. Extending this subsidiarity to his use of synods, he has repeatedly shown a special pastoral concern for the family, the domestic church that remains the foundational structure of *communio* centuries after the apostolic age, but under the contemporary pressures of rising divorce rates and irregular marital situations strains to confront the intergenerational challenges of faith transmission that chapter 1 described. Accompaniment of families in difficult situations, in dialogues open to hearing their genera-

---

72. Chris Lowney, *Pope Francis: Why He Leads the Way He Leads* (Chicago: Loyola Press, 2013), 118.

tional and cultural perspectives without any pre-judgment, has become a pastoral touchstone of this pope's highly participative understanding of Church as *communio*.

Francis further applies his image of "journeying together" on pilgrimage to the restlessness of digitalized youth, calling for a synodal way of interacting with them. To reach young people, the Church must move with them in a spirit of missionary flexibility, not cling to comfortable habits. In his post-synodal apostolic exhortation on youth, Francis demands a restless "pastoral care that is synodal," calling explicitly for "a participatory and co-responsible Church" of unity in diversity as he quotes the Final Document of the synod fathers:

> Youth ministry has to be synodal; it should involve a "journeying together" that values "the charisms that the Spirit bestows in accordance with the vocation and role of each of the Church's members, through a process of co-responsibility. . . . Motivated by this spirit, we can move towards a participatory and co-responsible Church, one capable of appreciating its own rich variety, gratefully accepting the contributions of the lay faithful, including young people and women, consecrated persons, as well as groups, associations and movements. No one should be excluded or exclude themselves."[73]

So far, the magisterial literature reviewed in this chapter shows how Francis has advanced the work of his predecessors to retrieve *communio*, presenting synodality as the key expression of a "participatory and co-responsible Church" in which

---

73. Francis, Post-Synodal Apostolic Exhortation *Christus Vivit* [Christ is Alive], March 25, 2019, no. 206, http://w2.vatican.va/content/francesco/en/apost_exhortations/documents/papa-francesco_esortazione-ap_20190325_christus-vivit.html.

laypeople transition from passive consumers of packaged content into active evangelizers of collaborative dialogues. Reflecting the digital shift from prepackaged pronouncement to participatory dialogue, Francis has developed several elements of *communio*-as-synodality (solidarity, collegiality, subsidiarity, co-responsibility, charity, and authenticity) with an innovative leadership style that promotes personal witness, fellowship, consultation, and accompaniment as key evangelization skills in a digital age. He has led by example, embodying the theological foundations of participatory conversation essential to any online faith-sharing initiative.

Francis calls all Catholics clergy and lay, young and old to collaborate with him in this mission of outreach as part of their baptismal calling. This call requires Catholic evangelizers in a digital age to rethink how they approach young people in group interactions offline and online. To make the "synodal pastoral care" of emerging adults a reality in this digital age, especially as they continue to abandon institutional religion, Francis asks Catholic adults to stop preaching at young people and start inviting them into roles of co-responsible leadership that use social media to engage their peers more interactively: "As for *outreach*, I trust that young people themselves know how best to find appealing ways to come together. They know how to organize events, sports competitions and ways to evangelize using social media, through text messages, songs, videos and other ways. They only have to be encouraged and given the freedom to be enthused about evangelizing other young people wherever they are to be found."[74]

The spontaneous zeal of young people defies traditional media packaging, emerging more from interpersonal sharing

---

74. Ibid., no. 210.

than from scripted exchanges, and evokes the participatory style of interaction that online faith-sharing requires to succeed. Francis encourages this effort by developing *communio* beyond his papal predecessors, building on their good work in adapting the perennial Catholic message to the signs of the times. Francis speaks to the digital age as a brother who has begun to empower synods to collaborate actively with him on pastoral strategies. For example, he encouraged the Pan-Amazonian synod to speak its mind about indults to consider ordaining women as deacons and older men of proven virtue (so-called *viri probati*) as married priests in remote regions of the rainforest, insisting that every idea be on the table. Though he ultimately passed on these proposals in favor of calling for a stronger permanent diaconate and more formalized lay ministries for women, his openness to hearing them illustrated his persistent belief in the ability of synodality to bring people together in one community of respectful dialogue.

In all his synods, Francis retains hierarchy, but softens it to hear the perspectives he needs to lead wisely. His decentralizing trend to redirect pastoral questions away from the dogmatically oriented CDF and toward synods may thus represent a fuller implementation of the ecclesiology of *communio* that popes since Vatican II have retrieved from apostolic Christianity as a theological foundation for a more participatory and co-responsible Church. His emphasis on diversity in unity can also fruitfully informs the digitally enabled faith groups that arise on social networks as initiatives of the New Evangelization, a final theological foundation of this project that the post-conciliar popes have developed in their magisterial teachings.

From Evangelization to New Evangelization

As we have seen, synods have become essential in telling the story of Catholicism's shift from packaged to participatory communication. But synodality unexpressed remains conceptual; it needs works of evangelization, or more precisely of the New Evangelization tailored to the "nones," to incarnate the sort of conversational faith communities it promises. That requires some understanding of the history and meaning of evangelization, and of the New Evangelization in particular, as a final theological foundation for online faith-sharing.

The English word "evangelization" comes from *evangelium*, the Latin word for "gospel" or "good news," and so the English word "evangelist" (proclaimer of the Gospel) originally referred to the four biblical authors Matthew, Mark, Luke, and John. In *Against the Heresies*, the second-century church father St. Irenaeus of Lyons, who claimed to have touched the apostolic age by hearing St. Polycarp speak of St. John the Apostle, relates how, even before written gospels existed, with a personal and communal joy the apostles proclaimed the Gospel to people who had not yet heard of Jesus. In book 3, chapter 1.1, Irenaeus recalls the first evangelization of the apostles arising from youthful zeal for what they shared:

> First they proclaimed it publicly and subsequently, by the will of God, handed it down to us in the Scriptures to be the foundation and support of our faith. It is wrong to assert that the apostles preached before their own knowledge was perfect, as some persons boast that they improve on the apostles. After our Lord rose from the dead, when the Holy Spirit came down upon them, the apostles were invested with power from on high; they were filled with all his gifts; they had per-

fect knowledge. Then they went out to the ends of the earth; they preached the glad news of the good things which come to us from God; they proclaimed heaven's peace to humanity.[75]

Zeal to share faith through any medium possible characterizes this initial proclamation, expressed peacefully through a witness of gladness, and infuses the apostolic discourse with co-responsible and participatory qualities. Noting how this first evangelization began with proclamation of the Good News rooted in personal and communal witness before proceeding to catechesis as a second stage, the systematic theologian Cardinal Avery Dulles writes: "Because faith flowers into testimony, the theology of faith is inseparable from a theology of witness. All the truths of revelation draw their meaning and power from their relationship to Christ's redemptive action, which comes to expression in the Gospel, the *evangelium.*"[76]

Conversion as a fruit of this witness remains a key element of evangelization in *Ad Gentes,* where the Second Vatican Council urged Catholics to "spread everywhere the reign of Christ" on the basis of the Church as "a universal sacrament of salvation."[77] Because by 1962 mass communications had connected the world in a way that allowed Christian evangelists to reach most non-Christian countries, the Council revisited traditional images of European priests baptizing pagans

---

75. Irenaeus of Lyons, "Against the Heresies," in *The Holy Spirit*, ed. J. Patout Burns and Gerald M. Fagin, SJ, (Eugene: Wipf and Stock, 2002), 32.
76. Avery Cardinal Dulles, SJ, *Evangelization for the Third Millennium* (Mahwah: Paulist Press, 2009), 79.
77. Second Vatican Council, Decree *Ad gentes* [On the Mission Activity of the Church], Oct. 11, 1962, no. 1, http://www.vatican.va/archive/hist_councils/ii_vatican_council/documents/vat-ii_decree_19651207_ad-gentes_en.html.

by emphasizing evangelization as the whole Church's mission even in Christianized nations. The decree *Apostolicam Actuositatem* further noted a "manifold and pressing need" for laity to become active Catholic evangelizers, especially by serving as catechists in Christian regions with few clergy.[78] Much like the early Christians among Gentiles and Jews, this renewal of evangelization for the modern world focused on lay outreach to people who blurred the distinction between ministry *ad intra* and *ad extra*, prefiguring today's attention to the religiously unaffiliated "nones" and non-practicing believers.

Other post-conciliar developments pushed Catholic evangelization much further. In 1974, the Third Synod on Evangelization ("Evangelization in the Modern World") expanded on the Council's call to adapt the witness of faith to modern circumstances, endorsing a contextual perspective that demanded greater pastoral appreciation of cultural diversity. Summarizing the synod's findings, Paul VI argued in *Evangelii Nuntiandi* (December 8, 1975) that evangelization must "transpose" the Good News to different languages and cultures:

> Evangelization loses much of its force and effectiveness if it does not take into consideration the actual people to whom it is addressed, if it does not use their language, their signs and symbols, if it does not answer the questions they ask, and if it does not have an impact on their concrete life. But on the other hand, evangelization risks losing its power and disappearing altogeth-

---

78. Second Vatican Council, Decree *Apostolicam Actuositatem* [On the Apostolate of the Laity], Nov. 18, 1965, no. 1, http://www.vatican.va/archive/hist_councils/ii_vatican_council/documents/vat-ii_decree_19651118_apostolicam-actuositatem_en.html.

er if one empties or adulterates its content under the pretext of translating it; if, in other words, one sacrifices this reality and destroys the unity without which there is no universality, out of a wish to adapt a universal reality to a local situation.[79]

This principle of transposing the Christian message to diverse contexts, making a more flexible application to evangelization of *communio*'s unity in diversity, suggests how Catholics might ideally approach faith-sharing in a digital age. The truth remains the truth. But Catholics must adapt how they share their faith to the new media culture (language, signs, symbols, and lived reality) of a digitally networked world. If those evangelized in this process evangelize others, Paul VI says it will be because witnesses show them the way: "Modern man listens more to witnesses than to teachers, and if he does listen to teachers, it is because they are witnesses."[80]

Paul VI saw with unique foresight the need for these witnesses to evangelize the baptized faithful who no longer practice their faith.[81] In the year of three popes, 1978, a successor emerged who developed his call for "a new period of evangelization" to such Catholics,[82] establishing the last theological foundation of this project. After the death of Paul VI and the thirty-three-day reign of John Paul I, Karol Wojtyła ascended to a twenty-seven-year papacy, stamping the Catholic Church with his forceful emphasis on missionary outreach to the growing number of religiously disaffiliated people in historically Christian nations like his own Poland. On his first

---

79. Paul VI, *Evangelii Nuntiandi*, no. 63.
80. Ibid., no. 41.
81. Ibid., nos. 52-53; 56-57.
82. Ibid., no. 2.

papal trip home in 1979, John Paul II coined the phrase "new evangelization" to distinguish this focus on post-Christian societies from traditional outreach to pagan societies ignorant of Jesus. Preaching to his fellow Poles, the pope introduced this New Evangelization as he stood in the shadows of *Nowa Huta*, the so-called "New City" outside Krakow that atheistic Communist officials had designed as a workers paradise without God by forbidding houses of worship. (Before becoming pope, Archbishop Wojtyła supported the faithful in erecting a cross near this atheistic city, celebrating illicit Masses on the site of what became a shrine.) It was in this context of desiring to restore faith to his traditionally Catholic homeland under atheist rule that John Paul II said in his homily: "A *new evangelization* has begun, as if it were a new proclamation, even if in reality it is the same as ever."[83] He called it the evangelization of the third millennium, arising from the cross of *Nowa Huta* as a guiding beacon into the present century.

In 1983, John Paul II expanded on these remarks, telling Latin America's bishops: "La conmemoración del medio milenio de evangelización tendrá su significación plena si es un compromiso vuestro como obispos, junto con vuestro presbiterio y fieles; compromiso, no de re-evangelización, pero sí de una evangelización nueva. Nueva en su ardor, en sus métodos, en su expresión."[84] These words clarified his

---

83. John Paul II, Apostolic Pilgrimage to Poland, *Holy Mass at the Shrine of the Holy Cross, Homily of His Holiness John Paul II,* June 9, 1979, no. 1, http://w2.vatican.va/content/john-paul-ii/en/homilies/1979/documents/hf_jp-ii_hom_19790609_polonia-mogila-nowa-huta.html.

84. John Paul II, Apostolic Pilgrimage to Central America, *Discourse of the Holy Father John Paul II to the Assembly of CELAM,* March 9, 1983, no. 1, https://w2.vatican.va/content/john-paul-ii/es/speeches/1983/march/documents/hf_jp-ii_spe_19830309_assemblea-celam.html. The pope

idea of a New Evangelization for the third millennium, fulfilling his pledge to bring it from the cross of Communist Poland's suffering into the rest of the world. This New Evangelization was to be a collaboration of bishops, priests, and laity. Although he described it as the same proclamation of faith as traditional evangelization, he said it would not be a "re-evangelization" because it would be new in its "ardor," "methods," and "expression," adapting the traditional content of the faith to contemporary circumstances.

For John Paul II, the New Evangelization demands a renewed effort of the whole Church to share the Good News particularly in secularized nations like the United States, using all available media to reach the baptized who no longer practice. Prefiguring the emphasis of Pope Francis on reaching people at the margins of Catholic life, John Paul II saw new media as the next existential periphery of this outreach. In his 1988 exhortation *Christifideles Laici*, he calls the whole Church to enter this new media frontier where lay professionals take the lead:

> The world of the mass media represents a new frontier for the mission of the Church, because it is undergoing a rapid and innovative development and has an extensive worldwide influence on the formation of mentality and customs. In particular, the lay faithful's responsibility as professionals in this field, exercised both by individual right and through community initiatives and institutions, demands a recognition of all its values, and demands

---

calls here for a "new evangelization" in the third millennium, "not a re-evangelization," "new in its ardor, in its methods, and in its expression" (translation mine).

that it be sustained by more adequate resource materials, both intellectual and pastoral.[85]

This vision of co-responsible media collaboration between supportive clergy and lay professionals in the New Evangelization further informs how Catholics might share faith through digital media in a way that eventually appeals to the religiously unaffiliated. In his 1990 encyclical *Redemptoris Missio*, he stresses that traditionally Christian nations need the New Evangelization *ad intra* in order to credibly evangelize *ad gentes* those nations where Christians remain a minority: "The churches in traditionally Christian countries, for example, involved as they are in the challenging task of new evangelization, are coming to understand more clearly that they cannot be missionaries to non-Christians in other countries and continents unless they are seriously concerned about the non-Christians at home. Hence missionary activity *ad intra* is a credible sign and a stimulus for missionary activity ad extra, and vice versa."[86]

Reflecting these developments under John Paul II, the US bishops' document "Go and Make Disciples" (1992) updated the language of evangelization to address the ongoing de-Christianization of society after Vatican II. Choosing to "rephrase" Paul VI's understanding of evangelization as converting "the personal and collective consciences of people,"[87] the document declared that "evangelizing means bringing the

---

85. John Paul II, Post-Synodal Apostolic Exhortation *Christifideles Laici* [On the Vocation and the Mission of the Lay Faithful in the Church and in the World], Dec. 30, 1988, no. 44, http://w2.vatican.va/content/john-paul-ii/en/apost_exhortations/documents/hf_jp-ii_exh_30121988_christifideles-laici.html.

86. John Paul II, *Redemptoris Missio*, no. 34.

87. Paul VI, *Evangelii Nuntiandi*, no. 18.

Good News of Jesus into every human situation and seeking to convert individuals and society by the divine power of the Gospel itself."[88] The bishops here develop Paul VI's post-conciliar emphasis on forming people's collective moral compass, extending it to include the conversion of society that John Paul II talked about.

For the United States in particular, the diversity in unity of New Evangelization means including Protestants in spiritual conversations, exchanging personal and communal witness in faith-sharing rather than seeking to convert one another. In his 1999 exhortation *Ecclesia in America*, John Paul II insists on this ecumenical spirit of witness, supporting the decision of this online faith-sharing group to invite "Catholic media consumers" from all religious affiliations. With declining religious observance in secularized nations that survived Communism's fall, John Paul II's respect for evangelicals is evident: "The presence of other Christian communities, to a greater or lesser degree in the different parts of America, means that the ecumenical commitment to seek unity among all those who believe in Christ is especially urgent."[89]

Following the death of John Paul II, the New Evangelization has continued developing as an inspiration for new media evangelization, putting flesh on the bones of *commu-*

---

88. United States Conference of Catholic Bishops, *Go and Make Disciples: A National Plan and Strategy for Catholic Evangelization in the United States*, Nov. 18, 1992, no. 10, http://www.usccb.org/beliefs-and-teachings/ how-we-teach/evangelization/go-and-make-disciples/introduction_go_ and_make_disciples.cfm.

89. John Paul II, Post-Synodal Apostolic Exhortation *Ecclesia in America* [On the Encounter with the Living Jesus Christ: The Way to Conversion, Communion and Solidarity in America], Jan. 22, 1999, no. 14, http://w2. vatican.va/content/john-paul-ii/en/apost_exhortations/documents/hf_jp-ii_exh_22011999_ecclesia-in-america.html.

nio and synodality by pushing Catholics repeatedly to focus on forming communities of faith where dialogue centers on the common good rather than on private concerns. Presenting evangelization as a service of charity to society, Benedict XVI wrote in his 2005 encyclical *Deus Caritas Est* that the "entire activity of the Church is an expression of a love that seeks the integral good of man," one that "seeks to promote man in the various arenas of life and human activity."[90]

These words underscore that genuine Christian outreach always supports authentic human development above partisan interests in faith-based exchanges. In his 2009 encyclical *Caritas in Veritate,* Benedict says care for others represents "an essential element of evangelization," highlighting the importance that in online conversations Catholics share experiences of service as well as prayer: "Testimony to Christ's charity, through works of justice, peace and development, is part and parcel of evangelization, because Jesus Christ, who loves us, is concerned with the whole person."[91]

More specific to the New Evangelization, Benedict XVI's curia later tweaked the definition of that idea in a 2007 doctrinal note from the CDF, the office he had led under John Paul II. Responding to the challenges of pluralism and relativism that informed much of his papacy, the note contextualizes as a work of New Evangelization this project's hope of forming Catholics in a participatory style of faith-sharing for digital outreach to disaffiliated Catholics. It states: "In

---

90. Benedict XVI, Encyclical Letter *Deus Caritas Est* [God is Love], Dec. 25, 2005, no. 19, http://w2.vatican.va/content/benedict-xvi/en/encyclicals/documents/hf_ben-xvi_enc_20051225_deus-caritas-est.html.

91. Benedict XVI, Encyclical Letter *Caritas in Veritate* [Charity in Truth], June 29, 2009, no. 15, http://w2.vatican.va/content/benedict-xvi/en/encyclicals/documents/hf_ben-xvi_enc_20090629_caritas-in-veritate.html.

a wider sense, [evangelization] is used to describe ordinary pastoral work, while the phrase 'new evangelization' designates pastoral outreach to those who no longer practice the Christian faith."[92]

Benedict himself clarified this understanding of the New Evangelization in his 2010 exhortation *Verbum Domini* on the role of God's word in the Church's mission:

> In a number of cases, nations once rich in faith and in vocations are losing their identity under the influence of a secularized culture. The need for a new evangelization, so deeply felt by my venerable Predecessor, must be valiantly reaffirmed, in the certainty that God's word is effective. The Church, sure of her Lord's fidelity, never tires of proclaiming the good news of the Gospel and invites all Christians to discover anew the attraction of following Christ.[93]

Also in 2010, Benedict XVI's apostolic letter *Ubicumque et Semper* established the Pontifical Council for Promoting the New Evangelization, once again calling the church in progressively secularized societies like his native Germany to a "renewed missionary impulse, an expression of a new, generous openness to the gift of grace."[94] In 2012, Benedict then

---

92. Congregation for the Doctrine of the Faith, *Doctrinal Note on Some Aspects of Evangelization,* Oct. 6, 2007, no. 12, http://www.vatican.va/roman_curia/congregations/cfaith/documents/rc_con_cfaith_doc_20071203_nota-evangelizzazione_en.html.

93. Benedict XVI, Post-Synodal Apostolic Exhortation *Verbum Domini* [On the Word of God in the Life and Mission of the Church], Sept. 30, 2010, no. 96, http://w2.vatican.va/content/benedict-xvi/en/apost_exhortations/documents/hf_ben-xvi_exh_20100930_verbum-domini.html.

94. Benedict XVI, Apostolic Letter in the Form of *Motu Proprio Ubicumque et Semper* of the Supreme Pontiff Benedict XVI Establishing the Pontifical Council for the New Evangelization, Sept. 21, 2010, http://

called a Synod on the New Evangelization for October 7-28, appointing fellow theologian Archbishop Rino Fisichella as the first president of the new pontifical council. Fisichella, who continued in this role under Francis, wrote in a book after the synod that the New Evangelization calls Catholics to share their faith particularly in the secularized "mediapolis" or "authentic culture" of digital media: "For good and for bad, from wherever we look at this media world, it appears more and more like a modern marketplace from which the Christian cannot remain estranged. The language which is being built up through the new form of communication, therefore, deserves to be known, studied, and, insofar as this is possible, used, without betraying the message we bear, in view of fostering a clear and effective understanding of that message."[95] Like recent popes, he worries only about the potential of social media to betray the gospel by fueling individualism and egoism.

Like Francis, in the joy of connecting to a community beyond oneself Fisichella finds an antidote to the self-seeking individualism that can fragment rather than unite people online. Looking again to the origins of faith, Fisichella identifies the theological roots of evangelization in Old Testament references to announcing a message of joy and in New Testament references to the proclamation and teaching of Jesus. Historically, he notes Erasmus (1466-1536) likely coined the derivative verb "to evangelize" in describing a certain kind of early Lutheran fanaticism,[96] but even that phrase takes on a happy meaning when it unites rather than divides people.

---

w2.vatican.va/content/benedict-xvi/en/apost_letters/documents/hf_ben-xvi_apl_20100921_ubicumque-et-semper.html.
95. Rino Fisichella, *The New Evangelization: Responding to the Challenge of Indifference* (Leominster, England: Gracewing, 2012), 75-76.
96. Ibid., 17.

Benedict XVI never finished his report on the 2012 synod. After Benedict resigned the papacy in February 2013, Francis completed and published the encyclical *Lumen Fidei,* calling it the work of two popes. Francis then wrote the post-synodal apostolic exhortation *Evangelii Gaudium* for the Synod on the New Evangelization, calling upon all Catholics to go out from their comfort zones with renewed apostolic zeal: "The new evangelization calls for personal involvement on the part of each of the baptized. Every Christian is challenged, here and now, to be actively engaged in evangelization; indeed, anyone who has truly experienced God's saving love does not need much time or lengthy training to go out and proclaim that love."[97]

Just as the digital revolution has accelerated secular development of more participatory media, Francis has accelerated papal development of a more participatory church. He sees the New Evangelization calling Catholics to respond lovingly to the indifference of secularized Christians by reaching out, without "much time or lengthy training," as witnesses to God's love. To incarnate this faith-sharing retreat's witness to the New Evangelization, *communio,* and a synodal style of dialogue, a digital media project like the one described here requires two final theological sources: prayer material to spark participatory dialogue and leadership principles to help a facilitator guide the group toward more interactive exchanges.

---

97. Pope Francis, Apostolic Exhortation *Evangelii Gaudium* [The Joy of the Gospel], Nov. 24, 2013, no. 120, Holy See, https://w2.vatican.va/content/francesco/en/apost_exhortations/documents/papa-francesco_esortazione-ap_20131124_evangelii-gaudium.html.

Ignatius and the Spiritual Exercises

The New Evangelization remains an abstraction without a framework in which to implement it as a synodal expression of *communio*. For an online faith-sharing group like the one we created to form Catholic media consumers into one community, it needed reflection material that not only united people in conversation around a common vocabulary, but challenged them to go deeper in sharing their lives with each other. In terms of conversational and relational depth, Ignatian spirituality offers an ideal tool for this sort of New Evangelization initiative. After cannon fire wounded him in battle at Pamplona, St. Ignatius of Loyola (1491-1556) underwent a religious conversion. Inspired by the burning desire to know and do God's will in his life, and to live his inherited Catholicism more intentionally in commitments big and small, he was filled with zeal for sharing his prayer experiences with others. Emerging from his own anguished dialogues with God in a cave on the banks of the Cardoner River in Manresa, Spain, his *Spiritual Exercises* retreat manual challenges retreatants on a deep personal level to move from packaged to participatory conversation with themselves and others as well as with the divine.

Consider as an example the contemplation on the Incarnation from #101-109 of the *Exercises*, a text participants reflected on in this faith-sharing project, where Ignatius asks retreatants to imagine the Holy Trinity gazing from heaven on the whole surface of the earth. Here the Triune God sees all the earth's diverse peoples struggling to survive and going down to hell as they hurt each other on purpose. As God contemplates this world that he gives up his only Son to save, Ignatius asks retreatants to imagine the Holy Trinity sending the Second Person to become human as Jesus, taking flesh in the womb of the Virgin Mary. Peering with God at the messy human relations of their own time and place, St. Ignatius invites retreatants in this exercise during the Second Week of his four-week structure to ask for the grace of "an intimate knowledge of our Lord, who has become man for me, that I may love Him more and follow Him more closely" (#104).[98] As with all key exercises of the retreat, the ensuing silent contemplation ends with Ignatius inviting retreatants to talk with God in a colloquy, apply the subject matter to their own lives, and share any thoughts or feelings that arose during the hour of prayer. Far from being a solely privatized religious experience, exercitants making the retreat individually will discuss their prayer over such texts (including more often the Scriptures themselves) with a spiritual director daily. On a preached group retreat, as this Facebook project replicated, they may instead talk about their prayer experiences with a faith-sharing group each day.

The basic evangelizing arc of the *Exercises* invites each person to move from focusing on oneself (one's needs, sinfulness, struggles, etc.) to placing God and the good of others at the center of one's awareness. As this participatory shift unfolds gradually in conversational engagement with God, others, and oneself, Ignatius fulfills McLuhan's embodied criteria for high participation dialogue by asking retreatants to use their imaginations to place themselves in the scenes of his freely composed exercises and in various Gospel passages. He invites retreatants throughout the *Exercises* to imagine what

---

98. St. Ignatius of Loyola, *The Spiritual Exercises of St. Ignatius: Based on Studies in the Language of the Autograph,* Translated by Louis J. Puhl, SJ (Chicago: Loyola Press, 1951), 49.

it looks, sounds, smells, tastes, and feels like to accompany Jesus as disciples. Evangelization unfolds in the *Exercises* primarily through the spiritual conversations (including the "colloquy" with God or a saint that ends each exercise, as well as regular chats with one's spiritual guide or group) they facilitate, "converting" the retreatant's heart in the sense of uniting it more deeply in communion with God, others in the person's life, and oneself.

During the sixteenth century, most of the people Ignatius led through these *Exercises* were not unbaptized Gentiles and Jews like the recipients of the first apostolic proclamation. Like himself, they were Catholics in various stages of affiliation whose "conversion" meant more deeply integrating their diverse individualities within the unity of their inherited faith community, rather than making a formal decision to become Roman Catholic. Indeed the spiritual conversations of the *Exercises* reflect the dialogical search for God of Ignatius himself, a nominal Catholic who in his pre-conversion life enjoyed gambling and womanizing more than churchgoing. As an ideal candidate for New Evangelization long before the term was even coined, after being crippled in battle Ignatius rose from his sickbed to become a respected founder who led recruits through the *Exercises* and during the age of exploration sent zealous priests of his missionary religious order to evangelize new lands. In this work he displayed certain leadership qualities that Pope Francis, his spiritual son, also models in his approach to evangelization and synodality as an expression of *communio*. Ignatian literature reveals three key leadership virtues to help facilitators encourage synodal dialogue in an outreach like this Facebook faith-sharing group: gratitude, self-awareness, and listening.

Conclusion: Ignatian Leadership Qualities

In going back to Scripture for his *Exercises*, St. Ignatius recaptured the participatory style of dialogue with God and others that marked the first evangelists. Ignatius stresses gratitude as a fundamental biblical theme of the first and last weeks of the *Exercises*, and one cannot overstate the importance of gratitude as a key leadership virtue in Ignatian spirituality. Gratitude begins (in the Principle and Foundation, #23) and ends (in the Contemplation to Attain Divine Love, or *Contemplatio,* #230) the *Exercises* as a grace of the relational style one learns from conversing with Jesus Christ, others, and oneself. Gratitude appears this way in the writings of Joseph Tetlow, a Jesuit theologian who once worked as the international assistant for Ignatian spirituality to former Jesuit superior general (1983-2008) Peter-Hans Kolvenbach, supervising more than two hundred retreat houses and spirituality centers worldwide. In a book on the foundations of Ignatian spirituality, Tetlow writes of the *Contemplatio* that closes the *Exercises*:

> Everything you have and are is God's gift. The whole universe, and everything in it, is a gift given. And God's giving continues, since all things are continually coming to be—and not only things, like rain and music, but also happenings, like a phone call or a visit with a friend. Here is the deepest foundation for the desire that spiritual people feel to give themselves and everything back to God. The yearning is not a kind of self-murder or abasement; it is desiring to love in the way of God, who gives and gives.[99]

---

99. Joseph A. Tetlow, SJ, *Making Choices in Christ: The Foundations of Ignatian Spirituality* (Chicago: Loyola Press, 2008), 119-120.

Tetlow captures well the mutuality of gratitude that can shine forth relationally in a participatory communications medium like Facebook. Ignatian leaders like Francis, formed by the full thirty-day *Exercises* as a standard part of their Jesuit training, model how to give and receive in this way. Facilitating an online faith-sharing group, Ignatian leaders steeped in the practice of grateful spiritual conversations strive to be comfortable enough to act with a spirit of authentic sharing, not of one-sided control.

Besides gratitude, the corporate leadership consultant Chris Lowney sees self-awareness as another leadership virtue St. Ignatius insisted on for Jesuits as a fruit of the *Exercises*, one that any facilitator of an online Ignatian faith-sharing retreat will want to practice. A former Jesuit seminarian himself, Lowney calls the *Exercises* the "key self-awareness tool" of Ignatius. He adds that Ignatian leaders teach this virtue self-awareness most effectively through their own behavior as spiritual guides in communal settings: "Leaders 'finger the vein' for others: their children, employees, coworkers, and friends. But first they make their own lifelong commitment to pursue self-awareness. All leadership begins with self-leadership, and self-leadership begins with knowing oneself."[100]

Francis, the world's most visible Jesuit, integrates the gratitude and self-awareness of his synodal media style within a third quality of Ignatian leadership that will help an online faith-sharing moderator: the ability to listen to every aspect of people's experience, even at the risk of unsettling those who feel content with the status quo, and to prioritize accompaniment over speaking during difficult conversations. In his sec-

---

100. Chris Lowney, *Heroic Leadership: Best Practices from a 450-Year Old Company That Changed the World* (Chicago: Loyola Press, 2003), 97-98.

ond book on Ignatian leadership, Lowney takes Pope Francis as his subject, stating the premise that leaders operate out of principles formed long before taking on their public roles. He devotes six chapters to the leadership habits he says Francis acquired from his long Jesuit formation in the spiritual ideals of St. Ignatius: Know oneself deeply; live to serve others; immerse oneself in the world; withdraw from the world daily; live in the present with reverence for tradition (gratitude); and create the future.

Noting how each pair of habits verges on contradiction, Lowney sees Francis holding these paradoxes together in "dynamic tension" through his Ignatian approach to discerning God's will for the long term amid the conflicts of the present. In the tradition of the *Exercises*, discernment primarily consists of listening for God's voice speaking through one's experiences, even if it creates paradox. While unilateral leaders may view the habit of praying before making decisions as weakness, creating too much unpredictability for people who expect unvarying routine, Lowney sees it helping Francis: "Well, there is something paradoxical and challenging about leading in this era of complexity and tumultuous societal changes. Leaders need the good judgment to distinguish, for example, between an inviolable organizational value that can never be changed and a once-useful tradition that now must change."[101]

For Francis, this ability of a listener to hold things in tension without judging or resolving them applies to others as well as to God. In Ignatian spirituality, a necessary fruit of the *Exercises* becomes the ability to hear God speaking through others, even when their words come across as unsettling or

---

101. Lowney, *Pope Francis,* 10.

challenging. Just as in the digital world of social media, good leaders of an Ignatian faith-sharing group remain open to adaptation and necessary change, but only after sitting with what they hear others saying. Repeatedly advising Catholics to practice an "apostolate of the ear," Francis radiates this Ignatian openness to hearing new things, especially in these words from his 2019 exhortation on holiness:

> Complacency is seductive; it tells us that there is no point in trying to change things, that there is nothing we can do, because this is the way things have always been and yet we always manage to survive. By force of habit we no longer stand up to evil. We "let things be", or as others have decided they ought to be. Yet let us allow the Lord to rouse us from our torpor, to free us from our inertia. Let us rethink our usual way of doing things; let us open our eyes and ears, and above all our hearts, so as not to be complacent about things as they are, but unsettled by the living and effective word of the risen Lord.[102]

Francis stresses how Ignatian leadership requires an attitude of open eyes, ears, and heart to whatever God offers. A good Ignatian guide accordingly approaches an online faith-sharing retreat group with a basic orientation toward listening for God speaking in others, a preference for hearing before talking that builds up trust. Jesuit William Barry, an expert spiritual director, notes: "Relationships develop only when the persons involved pay attention to one another."[103]

---

102. Francis, Apostolic Exhortation *Gaudete et Exultate* [Rejoice and Be Glad], March 19, 2018, no. 137, Holy See, http://w2.vatican.va/content/francesco/en/apost_exhortations/documents/papa-francesco_esortazione-ap_20180319_gaudete-et-exsultate.html.
103. William A. Barry, SJ, and William J. Connolly, SJ, *The Practice of Spiritual Direction* (New York: HarperOne, 2009), 48.

By employing these qualities of Ignatian spirituality, a group of people engaged in an online faith-sharing retreat following the *Exercises* might experience a more participatory form of ecclesial dialogue than more packaged Catholic media might allow. For St. Ignatius, one must first be led to become a leader. People must first learn how to share their faith more authentically with other Catholics online before reaching out to people beyond the bubble. For the virtual faith-sharing process to be a self-aware expression of New Evangelization, a theological act of synodal *communio* manifesting a co-responsible and participative Church in the sharing of religious experiences, it is necessary to learn a new way of listening before speaking and lead by example.

From Packaged to Participatory Consciousness

So far, I have shared the stories of how the media and Christians have tried to adapt to the digital revolution. The Canadian philosophical theologian Bernard J. F. Lonergan, SJ offers a framework for understanding the deeper elements of the participatory shift of digital media and the pastoral need it creates for Christians from different generations to share their faith on social networks. Now I want to illustrate how this might be done, using the stories of the participants in an online faith-sharing retreat group. In doing so, I will share how Lonergan's insights helped me to design and implement our online faith-sharing group, sketching an overview of who participated and how each session unfolded.

This project's methodology and its pastoral results illustrate how online faith-sharing might benefit Christian communities and cultures today. Throughout September and October 2020, I moderated a *Spiritual Exercises* faith-sharing retreat group of seventy-four men and women from around the world who indicated their interest by responding to a survey. In cooperation with *America Media* it was hosted on Facebook as a "secret" discussion group of Catholic media consumers taken from among existing *America* Facebook group members, friends they themselves invited, and individuals from other Ignatian groups. After an initial month of orientation, over the next thirty days they participated in four seven-day sessions that included daily guided reflection videos with faith-sharing prompts, following the four "weeks" of the Ignatian *Exercises.* [104] The project began with a month-long preparatory period of daily introductory videos and a pre-retreat survey; it ended with a transition video and post-retreat survey. Did the group answer the concern raised in chapter 2 that different generations interact digitally? Did it unfold in a participatory way? The rest of this chapter answers these questions in the affirmative, reflecting Lonergan's insights on how participants in such a group might have a religious experience and a conversion, organized in their understanding and sharing of material.

Lonergan's Pastoral Method

Lonergan's pastoral method elaborates a way of coming to authentic consciousness by attending to the structures of knowing, a process based in conversation. The framework for knowledge and communication that Lonergan proposes in *Insight* and in *Method in Theology* includes four transcendental precepts that explain pastorally how online-faith sharing could be fruitful for Catholics as an act of evangelizing dialogue outside of in-person settings.[105] By paying attention to

---

104. Facebook offers three kinds of groups: public, closed, and secret or private. Any user may find and join a public group by clicking into it. Anyone may also find a closed group but must ask to join it and await moderator approval. Secret groups remain invisible to the general population on Facebook, with users being able to join only by receiving and accepting a direct invitation from the administrator. After an initial month as a closed group with an invitation posted in other groups, *America's* editors suggested making this group secret for the sake of privacy.

105. For Lonergan, these epistemological innate norming processes are "transcendental" insofar as they lift people out of their subjectivity, with the self as a knowing subject seeking itself through personal appropriation of one's

experience and reflecting on it through conversation, Lonergan contends that subjectivity can become authentic—a process whereby the conscious self comes to terms with external realities—insofar as participants embrace four key tasks: being attentive, intelligent, reasonable, and responsible about their knowledge. These four precepts serve to describe the significance and role of religion when enacted through social media, as Lonergan implies in *Method in Theology*.[106]

By knowing their religious experience through self-reflection and testing its authenticity through conversation, retreatants in a faith-sharing group can base their judgments on shared insights about the true and the real. Yet Lonergan cautions that inattention, obtuseness, unreasonableness, and irresponsibility can lead to inauthenticity and alienate individuals from their true being—a cognitive bias that might come about if someone engages a retreat as an isolated individual who simply sits and thinks about things without conversing

---

own rational self-consciousness. In the context of this project, that makes the relationship with oneself (the self-knowledge revealed in faith-sharing questions) essential to grow in relationship with God and others.

106. "They are the radical intending that moves us from ignorance to seek what we do not know yet. They are unrestricted because answers are never complete and so only give rise to still further questions. They are comprehensive because they intend the unknown whole or totality of which our answers reveal only part. So intelligence takes us beyond experiencing to ask what and why and how and what for. Reasonableness takes us beyond the answers of intelligence to ask whether the answers are true and whether what they mean really is so. Responsibility goes beyond fact and desire and possibility to discern between what truly is good and what only apparently is good. So if we objectify the content of intelligent intending, we form the transcendental concept of the intelligible. If we objectify the content of reasonable intending, we form the transcendental concepts of the true and the real. If we objectify the content of responsible intending, we get the transcendental concept of value, of the truly good." Bernard J.F. Lonergan, SJ, *Method in Theology* (Toronto: University of Toronto Press, 1990), 11-12.

directly with God or another person. Lonergan reinforces the importance in a social media setting of providing opportunities for engaged interaction. Therefore this project's *Spiritual Exercises* retreat encouraged people to share their faith with each other in a Facebook group, posting their responses to evocative questions rather than merely reflecting upon the daily videos in isolation.

Within the exchange of teaching and learning that conversation partners experience in a group, Lonergan sees that personal witness (recalling the definition of evangelization in chapter 1 as the sharing of one's faith in Christ) helps them share the communal wisdom and common sense of their traditions. The ensuing interpersonal exchange of perspectives challenges their individual biases. In a key passage from his 1957 book *Insight,* Lonergan describes conversation as the engine that drives diverse individuals to achieve an authentic unity of consciousness. This excerpt offers a pastoral grounding for using digital media to unite people:

> Talking is a basic human art. By it each communicates to others what he knows, and at the same time provokes the contradictions that direct his attention to what he has overlooked. Again, far more impressive than talking is doing. Deeds excite our admiration and stir us to emulation. We watch to see how things are done. We experiment to see if we can do them ourselves. We watch again to discover the oversights that led to our failures. In this fashion the discoveries and inventions of individuals pass into the possession of many, to be checked against their experience, to undergo the scrutiny of their further questions, to be modified by their improvements. By the same token, the spontaneous collaboration of individu-

als is also the communal development of intelligence in the family, the tribe, the nation, the race. Not only are men [sic] born with a native drive to inquire and understand; they are born into a community that possesses a common fund of tested answers, and from that fund each may draw his variable share, measured by his capacity, his interests, and his energy.[107]

Emphasizing the communal "development of intelligence" that unfolds in the "spontaneous collaboration of individuals" within a group setting, Lonergan offered me a methodological grounding to lead the online faith-sharing group into a more interactive exchange about their religious experiences of the distinctive material of the *Exercises*. As members of this Ignatian faith-sharing group became comfortable logging on to view a daily video and post comments below it in response to reflection prompts, they shared wisdom about how to integrate the online experience into their offline routines. This process let them build communal intelligence from their different generational and other cultural lenses, implicitly and unconsciously developing unity rather than division by interacting freely as active partners. In Lonergan's terms, "be attentive" in this group referred to what the internet allowed participants to do on an unparalleled level as they got exposed to the thoughts and impressions of others; "be intelligent" connoted the questions they considered as part of their prayer experience; "be reasonable" meant the conclusions or judgments people came to as a result of the exchanges; and "be responsible" denoted the changed behaviors they evinced as a result of participating.

---

107. Bernard J.F. Lonergan, SJ, *Insight: A Study of Human Understanding* (New York: Harper and Row, 1978), 175.

Lonergan also emphasizes the imaginative content that could form the subject of knowledge and communication in an online retreat. In his *Exercises* St. Ignatius proposes the use of sensory imagination to contemplate the rich imagery of the Bible itself, elaborating on it with his own freely composed narrative scenes. In a 1965 address at Marquette University Lonergan suggests how a group of retreatants praying with their imaginations over gospel stories in this way could learn an authentic felt knowledge of reality:

> From the affect-laden images within us and from the many interpretations that illuminate them, one may turn outward to the phenomenology of intersubjectivity. Human communication is not the work of a soul hidden in some unlocated recess of a body and emitting signals in some Morse code. Soul and body are not two things but coprinciples in the constitution of a single thing. The bodily presence of another is the presence of the incarnate spirit of the other; and that incarnate spirit reveals itself to me by every shift of eyes, countenance, color, lips, voice, tone, fingers, hands, arms, stance. Such revelation is not an object to be apprehended. Rather it works immediately upon my subjectivity, to make me share the other's seriousness or vivacity, ease or embarrassment, joy or sorrow; and similarly my response affects his subjectivity, leads him on to say more, or quietly and imperceptibly rebuffs him, holds him off, closes the door.[108]

To be intelligent and reasonable about sharing one's interpretation of religious imagery entails a questioning that

---

108. Bernard J.F. Lonergan, SJ, "Dimensions of Meaning," 1965, in *The Lonergan Reader*, ed. Mark D. Morelli and Elizabeth A. Morelli (Toronto: University of Toronto Press, 1997), 398.

leads to the foundations of judgment, a conversion of consciousness. Lonergan uses conversion as a systematic thread in *Method in Theology,* citing Paul's words in Romans 5 that "the love of God has been poured out into our hearts through the holy Spirit that has been given to us" as a key turning-point in that work.[109] This project could not presume or prove that online retreatants experienced a fundamental religious conversion of this kind. But in the daily faith-sharing prompts, as well as in surveys before and after the retreat, it did ask participants to self-report their sense of growing in the graces Ignatius proposes for each week of his *Exercises* retreat that begins and ends in God's love.[110] Keeping conversion in mind as a hoped-for outcome of evangelization, the project did seek to elicit a shift of consciousness for retreatants, disposing them better for deeper spiritual movements.

Working Within a Digital Culture

So how did this project contribute to the intergenerational and ecclesial challenges raised in relation to the participatory use of digital media for evangelization? But, more personally, how do we ordinary believers enter into this story of digital media? The good news is that we are already a part of this story if we use social networks; we then need only enter into the story of Christian attempts to use it by participating more intentionally in faith-based outreach. It will help now to consider some best practices for this outreach and reflect on the story of this

---

109. Romans 5:5. For the sake of consistency, this citation comes from the same Bible translation used in earlier chapters. Lonergan paraphrases this passage on p. 105 of *Method.*

110. The Ignatian retreat begins with the First Principle and Foundation (no. 23) and ends with the Contemplation to Attain the Love of God (no. 230). Appendix 1 indicates the dates this group reflected on these two exercises.

particular Facebook faith-sharing retreat group as one attempt to live them out.

Our faith-sharing retreat group based on the *Spiritual Exercises* was hosted on Facebook in collaboration with *America Media*, a US media ministry of the Society of Jesus. As a longtime Jesuit from the end of Generation X (born 1980), I brought my experiences of directing retreats and leading Catholics through offline faith-sharing groups. As someone who has used Facebook since 2007 for Catholic media work, I also brought a basic literacy with this platform that helped me face the challenge of adapting traditional Ignatian spirituality to a contemporary media setting. Gradually an adaptive design emerged for this electronic outreach that began with attentiveness to key principles of Christian culture and to secular literature about online group dynamics. The resulting design sought to help older Catholics familiar with faith-sharing culture, still very much the majority of people who participate in religious activities, better engage the social media culture of younger believers with no adult memories before cyberspace.

What definition best contains all the meanings of culture that I proposed for evangelization in this project? The sociologist Patricia Wittberg defines culture broadly as "what makes us human"[111]—a set of shared attitudes, values, goals, and practices that characterize an institution, organization, or group to help the people in it to discover meaning. She says of the millennials on social media: "They are digital natives: accustomed to personal computers, email, and cell phones from childhood, they spend more time online than they do watching."[112]

111. Patricia Wittberg, SC, *Catholic Cultures: How Parishes Can Respond to the Changing Face of Catholicism* (Collegeville: Liturgical Press, 2016), 2.
112. Ibid., 65.

In this sentence, Wittberg presents the key difference between traditional Christian culture and digital media culture as a distinction between "watching" something unfold as an interested spectator (the primary mindset of pre-digital communication) and the more participatory online interaction this project sought to encourage by adapting the high-participation *Exercises*. While millennial and post-millennial cultures have been formed by the participatory exchanges of the internet, which engage their judgment directly about what to take in or reject, twentieth-century Catholic parochial cultures in particular revolved around programmatic rituals (Mass, Eucharistic adoration, etc.) that resembled the relatively passive media consumption habits of that time. As a result of this disconnect, older believers who go online often find themselves a "cognitive minority" lacking the experiential language to engage digital interactions well, even as emerging adults lack the same fluency with traditional spirituality in offline religious settings.[113]

According to Wittberg, engaging both sides of this digital cultural divide with a sophisticated electronic outreach can paradoxically help believers of all ages connect with their shared need for quiet reflection and deeper interpersonal connections. She stresses that the burden lies more on older generations—who, with stable lives and relatively stronger ecclesial bonds, will be likeliest to dominate membership of a faith-based group even online—to learn online culture than on younger generations to learn traditional religious culture. Wittberg, a religious sister, observes of her own Christian community: "There remains a window of opportunity to strengthen

---

113. Ibid., 75.

these remaining, if tenuous, ties to the Catholic Church among millennials. But this window is closing."[114]

Based on these insights, my design for this online faith-sharing group arose from a conscious decision to be as flexible as possible for younger members, even as I remained mindful that a majority of participants would likely come from older generations with a focus on sharing their wisdom in a digital setting. As a potential obstacle to this intergenerational openness, Wittberg warns of a trend in contemporary culture toward "social desirability bias," whereby people consume only whatever content confirms their views to get along with peers rather than argue. This trend tends to segregate people among like-minded peers, excluding any generational minority. "We disproportionately pay attention to information that supports our point of view and resist information that disconfirms it," Wittberg writes, adding that links from friends and ideological news sources that Facebook tailors to people's online habits make it "less likely that we will even *hear* viewpoints which differ from our own."[115]

With that in mind, research into digital group dynamics revealed several best practices of online culture that challenge this social desirability bias, offering a basis for older generations to communicate online in a new way. First, online groups work better in a spirit of teamwork than of argumentative competition, perhaps distinguishing them from pre-digital communication. Five British medical education researchers found that online small group collaboration succeeds through its convenience, engagement, documentation, democratization, and social interaction: "It is important for potential online collab-

---

114. Ibid., 82.
115. Ibid., 56.

orators to be mindful of these and be aware of the plethora of online collaborative tools, each with their different attributes and limitations."[116] To foster such awareness in a way that stayed flexible for the younger participants in my Facebook group, I opted to set up this project as an asynchronous group, allowing global retreatants to log in at any time to follow and discuss daily video reflections rather than worry about participating on a fixed schedule with perfect internet connection. Predisposed to encourage conversation about prayer experiences, rather than the arguments that characterize much of online Christian interaction, I also chose the imaginative self-reflections of the *Exercises* over the more apologetic focus that some popular media evangelizers might prefer.

Second, this collaborative spirit fails to form in groups that do not talk openly about the online culture into which participants enter, and this failure to exercise critical judgment in relation to the experience itself may block authentic unity from forming. Researcher Namsook Jahng offers three quantitative indices of collaborative effectiveness during online discussion within a small group: quantity (number of words exchanged in the group), equality (participation variability among members), and shareness (team-spirit/teamwork measured by the portion of posts addressed to all group members). In a healthy group, Jahng says, online collaboration fosters a messy learning process that helps participants seek a new knowledge and interconnectedness rooted in sharing the same experience: "The goal and genuine outcome of a collaborative learning process can be said to be members' constructed knowledge.

---

116. Sarah Al-Amodi, "Collaborate Online As a Small Group," *Education for Primary Care* 26, no. 2 (2015): 129, https://doi: 10.1080/14739879. 2015.11494327.

Throughout the collaboration process, group members presumably have contributed to members' constructing knowledge as well as establishing group membership."[117]

As our online group grew in knowledge of Ignatian spirituality, I kept these factors in mind so as to better guide those participants who stayed for the entire retreat despite initially seeming to be passive, to lack spontaneity in their interactions, and to resist entering into the level of agreement necessary to form a community. They also helped me track the group's shrinkage down to a relatively small core of seventy-four post-retreat survey respondents, another essential principle of success with online groups. Research into online learning has shown that when participants get winnowed into smaller discussion groups to make discussions less "busy" and repetitive, group members begin to speak and think critically at a higher level.[118]

To help the group gradually self-select its final membership in this way, I used September 2020 as a preparatory discernment month, offering daily introductory videos and discussion prompts on the *Exercises*. This month gave invited members time to discern whether they wished to proceed and to invite friends to join. Accompanying group members in this discernment process, I observed how their engagement deepened in proportion to their commitment to continuing, and encouraged them to participate without pushing anyone

---

117. Namsook Jahng, "Collaboration Indices for Monitoring Potential Problems in Online Small Groups," *Canadian Journal of Learning and Technology* 39, no. 1 (Winter 2013): 5, https://doi: 10.21432/T2Z30Q.

118. Kerstin Hamann, Philip H. Pollock, and Bruce M. Wilson, "Assessing Student Perceptions of the Benefits of Discussions in Small-Group, Large-Class, and Online Learning Contexts," *College Teaching* 60 (2012): 67, https://doi: 10.1080/87567555.2011.633407.

to stay or go. Despite an initial period of hesitation and some members remaining silent throughout the thirty days, this positive encouragement ultimately helped a self-selecting core of more committed retreatants interact freely with each other in an open dialogue.

As social media communities form in this way, they develop settled ways of interacting unique to each one. In a study of online group formation and development, digital media researchers found that "shared repertoires" (common patterns in participant behaviors) emerge naturally when members come to understand and accept the reality of a new experience and begin to converse about it: "The more familiar the metaphors and tools are to participants, and the more intuitively adaptable the tools are, the more quickly community is able to form."[119] To make this process go smoothly, I also had to serve as a resource person. One study of problem-based learning by medical students in an online small group suggested that moderators be available to help participants with "particularly their usage of information technology to answer questions as they arise."[120] Such questions did arise particularly during this project's invitation month of daily introductory videos, when newcomers settled into the format and discussed how to integrate the Facebook tool set with their offline prayer habits and readings. Reading from my own devotional edition of the *Exercises* with explanations and faith-sharing prompts, I soon

---

119. Sean P. Goggins, James Laffey, Michael Gallagher, "Completely Online Group Formation and Development: Small Groups as Socio-Technical Systems," *Information Technology & People* 24, no. 2 (June 2011): 129, https://doi: 10.1108/09593841111137322.

120. Christopher B. Reznich and Elizabeth Werner, "Facilitators' Influence on Student PBL Small Group Session Online Information Resource Use: A Survey," *BMC Medical Education* 4, no. 1 (15 June 2004): 5, https://doi: 10.1186/1472-6920-4-9.

posted a free PDF file of the book after some people requested copies of what I was reading. I also posted a free online translation of the *Exercises*[121] among other resources.

Finally, successful online groups stay flexible about how discussion unfolds, allowing it to do so naturally rather than trying to control it or forcibly replicate offline interaction patterns. In an intensive study of how students progressed from multiple perspectives to a shared understanding of their research questions in a small online group, Kati Makitalo-Siegl found the nature of online discussion to be cyclical rather than linear, suggesting the futility of a facilitator trying to project rigid rules of order from offline groups onto a digital platform. Makitalo-Siegl observed the participatory value of this cyclical discussion in her study: "The learners' shared knowledge became the group's tacit knowledge, reused to build new understanding." [122]

With such flexibility in mind, I kept this retreat's daily live-stream reflection videos with faith-sharing prompts available for participants to access at any time, rather than insist on a series of tightly scheduled video chat meetings. Having all the recorded videos with conversation threads permanently available allowed participants from around the globe to follow multiple timelines (so that Day 30, despite being recorded on October 30, could occur whenever someone viewed that day's video) and share their responses to the material by posting or interacting at any time in the comment section below each

---

121. That would be the translation by Louis J. Puhl, quoted earlier in chapter 2 and listed later in the bibliography.

122. Kati Makitalo-Siegl, "From Multiple Perspectives to Shared Understanding: A Small Group in an Online Learning Environment," *Scandinavian Journal of Educational Research* 52, no. 1 (February 2008): 92, https://doi: 10.1080/00313830701786677.

video. In particular, younger participants with active families and jobs posted words of gratitude for this decision, because it allowed them amid busy routines to feel freer about following at their own pace and engagement level.

Description of Invited Participants

Collaborating with two fellow members of the *America Media* editorial staff as co-administrators of the Facebook group, I reached out to "Catholic media consumers" who consisted of existing *America* Facebook group members as well as young adults from Jesuit institutions. As a member of the *America* staff, I received special access to its Facebook page, allowing me to post an invitation (appendix B) to this new "Spiritual Exercises Faith-Sharing Retreat Group" in four existing closed discussion groups. In order to include people unfamiliar with *America's* platforms, I also invited members of my public Sean Salai Author Facebook page, as well as the SLU Catholic Studies Program Facebook page at Saint Louis University.

After the retreat concluded on October 31, I determined the following about the participants from Facebook's internal analytics Group Insights.[123] The group finished with 395 total members including active participants, the three Facebook group co-administrators, inactive observers who had not followed through on an initial intention to participate, and people who had ended up auditing after neither completing the pre-retreat survey to indicate full participation nor accepting my invitation to depart the group. Of that number, 212 people completed the pre-retreat survey indicating their interest

---

123. This information cannot be sourced with a web link because it remains internal to the group's confidential page.

in following the entire retreat, and on October 2 the group hit a peak of 277 members engaging the content. The retreat concluded with 139 members engaging the last post on October 30. Of those who ended up participating in discussion and completing the full retreat, the aforementioned seventy-four finished the post-retreat survey.

Even with this gradual self-selection process that narrowed the retreat down to these active participants and a broader swath of semi-engaged auditors, the strong privacy settings and etiquette policies of Facebook ensured a safe space for sharing. The vast majority of people who remained in the group fell into comfortable patterns of participation, engaging the faith-sharing prompts most often during weekend nights. Facebook group analytics showed that the most popular times for members to post, comment, or react to the daily video posts in both September (introductory period) and October (the retreat proper) turned out to be 6 pm on Saturdays and 9 pm on Sundays, US Central Time. The evening proved more active than in the mornings, when at members' request I live-streamed all videos and left them posted with introductory texts that contained the verbal discussion prompts.

Also at the request of members, the group remained secret and active after the retreat. That allowed participants to continue using it for ongoing interpersonal interactions or to complete the retreat on their own time, and protecting the privacy of personal things they had shared by not opening it to new members. It also spoke to the depth of their sharing.

All of this data implies that participants in our retreat shared an active, healthy, and productive social media experience as defined by McLuhan's participatory criteria and the social media literature quoted previously in this book. Reinforcing that indication from an etiquette standpoint, Facebook did not flag any violations of its community standards or censor any posts for what it calls "false news," and participants made no report of any negative interactions to the moderator or the group at large. Despite coming from 101 cities on six continents, both passive and active members stayed respectful of each other, sharing experiences rather than opinions.

Generationally, Facebook confirms that no one under the age of eighteen participated in the group as silent or active members, and a good mix of genders and locations coexisted. Of the 390 people total who existed in the group as participants or auditors at some point, 146 (37 percent) were men and 244 (63 percent) were women, reinforcing the anecdotal observation that women tend to be more willing to participate in Catholic-themed Christian spirituality groups.

Stories from Retreatants

Our "Spiritual Exercises Faith-Sharing Retreat Group" began on September 30 with a month-long period of invitation, introductory videos, discussions, and a pre-retreat survey; continued with the thirty-day retreat of half-hour daily videos with faith-sharing prompts; and concluded in a farewell video on October 31, with daily invitations through November 7 to take a post-retreat survey. Because a secret group does not allow people to apply to join it, this one started as a closed group until September 30, allowing people to join and introduce themselves as well as take the pre-retreat survey posted under announcements. It also allowed members to invite friends not included in the original invitation, including some newcomers to Ignatian spirituality. Throughout September I posted daily introductory videos, orienting participants to the digital format and flow of the retreat as well as to the

Exercises proper.[124] As the group received relevant data during this month-long preparation for the retreat, I invited people to post introductions and get to know each other, using the videos to help discern whether they felt called to take the pre-retreat survey and move ahead with the thirty-day faith-sharing retreat in the proposed format.

For each day's live-streamed guided video, I used a 2020 devotional edition of the *Exercises,* to which I had added reflection materials so as "to share the text more generously" among people who can't easily pray through it in a traditional retreat house setting. In my role as moderator, to the September videos I adapted supplementary material from St. Ignatius on preparing for a retreat, inviting discussion of faith-sharing prompts and feedback on the digital format in the comment box below each video.[125] That set the pattern of the October retreat videos as well.

The videos during the introductory month posed questions that encouraged retreatants to be intelligent about the supplemental materials of St. Ignatius on topics like prayer routines, penance, eating, the saint's own introductory notes to the *Exercises,* spiritual reading for the time of retreat, and the saint's recommendations for different parts of the four-week structure. For example, the September 13 video on St. Ignatius's subtitle (#21) to the *Exercises* drew eighteen participant remarks. I offered a "prelection" explanation, then proposed some faith-sharing reflection prompts for people to share

---

124. A detailed timeline of topics for all videos posted in the September pre-retreat period and October's thirty-day retreat period with post-retreat day will be found in Appendix 1.
125. St. Ignatius Loyola, *The Spiritual Exercises of St. Ignatius of Loyola: With Points for Personal Prayer from Jesuit Spiritual Masters,* ed. Sean Salai, SJ (Charlotte: TAN Books, 2020), xxxii.

about in the comment section: "What compulsive fixations leave me feeling disconnected from God, myself, and others? What helps me to stop obsessing over sin and focus instead on Jesus at the center of my awareness? What do I want from God that might help me with that?"[126] In response, one woman, a Louisiana Baby Boomer born in 1949, shared the desire for connection that she brought to the group: "The questions on this video exactly target my long-standing feeling of unease and disappointment with myself for living my live in a very 'detached from others' way. Thanks for offering this retreat prep. You give me hope that if I honestly apply myself to this process, God might guide me toward a more deeply-felt caring for others."[127] This comment typified the yearning for connection that brought people into the group, and their willingness to confront any obstacles to their relationships with God, themselves, and others.

During the first seven-day session of daily reflection videos, the *Exercises* challenged participants to seek greater self-knowledge of the brokenness in their relationships caused by such obstacles, inviting each to pray for the first week grace of St. Ignatius to grow in "a deeply felt sense of God's love for me, even though I am a sinner."[128] In the October 7 video that drew fifty-two comments, I read a guided meditation on death. Based on #71 from the *Exercises,* it included a preliminary explanation that quoted from a letter of St. Ignatius on God's

---

126. Ibid., 11.
127. Please note that because this group remains private, i.e. not accessible to the public, no web address can be cited for these anonymous quotes of faith-sharing comments. Participants gave explicit permission to use these quotes.
128. This wording comes from the pre-retreat and post-retreat questionnaires, reprinted in appendix 2, which chapter 4 will show asked specific questions about each of the four graces St. Ignatius proposes.

love and offered context from the saint's life story. Before and after reading this guided imaginative meditation, in which I gave the usual Ignatian instructions for settling into a prayerful bodily posture with deep breathing to ensure the sort of embodied engagement that McLuhan insists upon, I invited retreatants to post comments below the video on these faith-sharing prompts: "How have I failed to trust in God's love by trying to force perfection in my life according to my own timeline or designs? What deceptive thoughts keep me from accepting myself in all of my messiness as a loved sinner? What helps me accept God's unconditional love for me?"[129]

During the live stream, as I paused between these questions and the text of the exercise, an eighty-one-year old Illinois man from the Silent Generation made this comment that received an appreciative reaction (i.e., the thumbs up emoji) for its generational wisdom: "When I was growing up and on into the late 1970's the Church emphasized doing good and avoiding evil. It was Pelagian. I thought I needed to earn brownie points with God. I needed to earn God's love. I now accept totally that God does love me, even in my sinfulness. It's freeing on a spiritual level. It actually motivates me to love." This man's comment displayed attentiveness to the material, intelligence about the questions it raised, reasonableness in the judgment he reached about God's unconditional love, and responsibility in his desire to love in the same way.[130]

Between October 8 and 14, I presented seven daily video reflections on the second week theme of following Christ,

---

129. Ibid., 62.

130. For people wishing more material to pray over, I also shared suggested additional readings from the translation in my edition of the book (in this case Mt 25:31-46 and *The Imitation of Christ* book 3, chapter 14) and continued to do so during the four seven-day sessions of the retreat proper.

praying for the grace of Ignatius that each person might grow in a desire to accompany Jesus and labor with him in his ongoing ministry. On October 8, the Day 8 video (the days always matched the dates on this retreat, making it easier for people to find old videos if they fell behind) drew fifty-one comments. I read a guided meditation on the Call of the King exercise (#91), in which St. Ignatius invites retreatants to contemplate Jesus as the one who calls them to follow him. As always, I added suggested readings for those who desired more material for personal prayer. After reflecting on the video and praying however they pleased over the material, participants shared on the following questions: "What qualities of leadership do I see in Jesus Christ? To what sort of 'kingdom' does Christ the King call me? If I were to imagine a Christlike political leader today who called me to assist in establishing a more just world, what might that person look and sound like?"[131]

A millennial mother and wife born in 1985, who works for a US Catholic diocese, responded by emphasizing judgment and action: "So much of this spoke to the depths of my heart where there is this desire to be a soldier for Christ. His crusader following Him into battle to fight for souls. He never sends me alone but always goes before me. He leads by first taking on every pain, suffering, unknown there is. . . but never for no reason. His vulnerability, mercy, servant leadership has never been without purpose. He does it for me. For you. For souls."

During this second session of seven daily faith-sharing videos, I invited participants to take up some spiritual reading or movie and think about any decision or particular grace they wished to bring to prayer during the retreat. A millennial

131. Ibid., 87.

woman from the Philippines spontaneously started an October 11 discussion thread (Day 11 of the retreat, on which I posted a video praying with the hidden life or childhood of Jesus from #132-134) to share that she was reading *The Cloister Walk* by Kathleen Norris. She shared a photo of the book in her post with these words, raising an intelligent community-building question: "What's everyone reading or watching for retreat? I am enjoying this book very much." The nineteen comments that ensued indicated the participatory success of the group up to that point. Moreover, participants continued throughout the retreat to share photographs and other media (including songs and poems) in spontaneous discussion threads that helped people feel more connected to the virtual community.

Amid the third seven-day session of daily videos, October 15-21, as retreatants prayed for the third week grace of Ignatius to experience a stronger desire to suffer compassionately with Jesus in his passion, I invited retreatants to use their imaginations to place themselves in the gospel stories of the passion using points provided by St. Ignatius in #261-312 for the last three weeks of the *Exercises*. On Day 20, October 20, I shared a guided contemplation on the death of Jesus using the points from #297 and Luke 23:39-49. In response to my invitation for participants to share where the Spirit led them in the exercise, where they encountered resistance, and what words or phrases struck them as they used their imaginations to place themselves in the scene, a millennial Latina single woman from Texas born in 1986 shared some aspects of religious conversion in her desire to suffer with Jesus:

> I sense the Holy Spirit leading me to stay in front of the cross with Mary Magdalene, Mary, St. John. We are where Jesus is hanged I stay there with them. I am at a

loss for words because in that moment filled with anger, tears, sadness and grief. We console each other in those emotions but in this meditation a point I ponder was no one comforts Jesus when he dies and is on the cross and that made me feel a connection to him when no one comforts me if I am sad, [in] pain. Jesus took it all. I found myself having resistance when we actually prayed the Our Father prayer, because he felt abandoned and still forgives those who have hurt him out of love. Love is stronger than death.... Another image I absolutely love is the blood and water flow when he gets pierced that is pure love and a love that is transformative, merciful, and a love that [is] cleansing and that makes me always want to be near him and with him in the midst of my sufferings and others who might be suffering.

The October 20 video that elicited this sharing drew only twenty-seven comments, signaling a phase of the retreat where some people struggled to enter the most painful stories or else fell behind and started catching up with the videos later. Conversely, as tends to happen in online groups, this period also brought the most active participants closer together as a smaller number interacted more deeply. On October 27, one woman started a discussion thread checking in with how people found themselves wrapping up the retreat. This prompted another woman, a Baby Boomer from the Chicago area born in 1959, to share that she had just returned to the retreat after dropping out for a while when a close family member had died. A third woman from the Philippines then shared that she had also fallen behind by two weeks and asked that the group remain active with the videos following the retreat, affirming the wisdom of making the group asynchronous due to the length of the commitment. Given the avowed invitation of the online retreat to be a "take what's needed and leave the rest" experience, focusing on relationships rather than tasks, I encouraged participants in daily videos at this point to not worry about finishing every video like a homework assignment but simply to reflect on what they had received where they did engage.[132]

During the fourth and final seven-day session, October 22 to 28, retreatants prayed for the fourth week grace of Ignatius to rejoice more deeply with the risen Jesus Christ in gratitude for all he had given them. On Day 24, October 24, the video drawing twenty-seven comments presented a guided contemplation with the points of St. Ignatius (#306) on what he numbers as the Eighth Apparition of the Risen Christ in Jn 21:1-25. Responding to an invitation to share where the Spirit guided her in this prayer, a single San Antonio woman from Generation X born in 1977 shared the following insight from her own self-knowledge: "As I hear about the disciples fishing, I am drawn to a modern image of me 'fishing' for good things in my life—perhaps the fruits of the Holy Spirit, particularly joy. I am unable to catch it on my own, but if I follow His way, my life may be overfilled with joy."

On October 29 and 30, the retreat concluded with two transition days focusing on how participants might shift from consciousness to action by taking the graces of the retreat back into their offline lives, as I posted videos on the Rules for Giving Alms (#337) of St. Ignatius to invite insights on how to serve the poor and his Rules for Thinking with the Church (#352) to invite participants to reflect on the quality of their

---

132. In response to my direct message inquiries during the retreat, several participants indicated they followed the daily videos without commenting on them, suggesting their desire to pray privately and helping to explain why a given video might have 150 views and only twenty-seven comments.

connection to a faith community outside the virtual space. In the Day 30 video presenting the latter rules with an introductory quotation from Pope Francis about them, posted October 30, I invited retreatants to reflect on their future connection to a worshipping community by posting their responses to these questions: "Which of these rules speak to my experience? Which of these rules challenge or confuse me? In what ways do I strive in my life to think with Holy Mother Church, rather than against her, even when I disagree with the actions of her leaders?"[133]

In response, a US-based wife and grandmother from the Silent Generation shared a glimmer of conversion insofar as the rules for thinking with the Church had challenged her to stay connected to the institutional Catholic community in the future, recognizing God's continuing presence there despite her ongoing doubts:

> I felt like I entered a time machine which took me back to Catholic grade school in the 50's and high school of the early 60's. With the exception of the direction of Mass, reception of Eucharist and Confession they all challenge me to flee the institutional Catholic Church. . . . I found the effect of Vatican 2 to be life giving and empowering. As a woman I saw hope in a Church who strove to see me as holy, worthy to be a participant rather than a somewhat needy recipient. . . . The continuing revelations about clergy abuse defeats the faithful efforts of our good, holy, and faith-filled priests and bishops. I take these feelings to prayer daily because I truly know that somehow our Loving God remains in our Church.

133. Ibid., 328.

On October 31, I shared a farewell and thank you video, encouraging people to keep using the group. I then invited participants to share any points of gratitude at the end of the retreat and to complete the post-retreat survey questionnaire pinned at the top of the group's announcements page, continuing to post daily reminder videos about it until November 7. Among the twenty-six comments posted by that evening, Halloween, one seventy-seven-year old New Jersey woman from the Silent Generation who had felt isolated by Covid-19 quarantines shared the following insight of gratitude: "I add my gratitude and thanks to all those thoughts expressed by others. This experience certainly has been a wonderful blessing especially during these difficult times. The sense of connection to God and to others added a special dimension to my life."

These quotations from participants of different generations and locations highlight the qualities of mutuality and unity that characterized this group, hinting at a participatory dialogue that drew people together amid their diverse perspectives ranging from Catholics who recall Vatican II and 1970s catechesis to younger people with more pietistic images of soldiering and suffering. By praying for the graces Ignatius proposes in the four weeks of the *Exercises*, retreatants learned a common language, practicing reasonable intending as they progressed from a shift of consciousness to the point of religious conversion. They found unity in diversity.

Conclusion: Conversion to God and Community

In a digital format this online retreat sought to create the conditions for participants to experience some shift toward God and community, however small those signs of hope might seem in the above description of design principles and narration of participant experiences. Accepting Lonergan's premise that listening to the word and communicating the word constitute two processes of theology, this retreat offered a digital mini-study of these two dimensions through which individuals overcome cognitive bias in a group setting: how people listen to the Word filtered through the *Exercises*, and how they communicate on the basis of the Word with each other. That process demands openness to conversion, a traditional evangelization goal.

For St. Ignatius, who wrote the *Exercises* during his own conversion from disaffiliated Catholic to zealous disciple, the purpose of his retreat will always include the conversion of heart that results from making a firm decision on the basis of one's experiences of God in prayer to know and do his will. For many of the members of this Facebook group, that decision arose from a deepening awareness of their desire for interpersonal connection, moving them from passivity to a more active desire to share their faith online as well as online. Chapter 4 will analyze the retreat surveys for signs of this movement; chapter 5 will then offer some tentative conclusions and recommendations for future digital outreach. The retreat could not and did not fully resolve all the issues these chapters have raised. It did make a full effort to address them and push an evangelizing response as far as it could go in the digital realm, within the limits this chapter sets out. The next two chapters will give reasons for this partial and limited effort to inspire more like it. As G.K. Chesterton once observed, "The Christian ideal has not been tried and found wanting. It has been found difficult; and left untried."[134]

---

134. Gilbert Keith Chesterton, "What's Wrong with the World," 1910, in *The Wisdom of Mr. Chesterton: The Very Best Quotes, Quips, & Cracks*, ed. Dave Armstrong (Charlotte: Saint Benedict Press, 2009), 167.

Lessons Learned
from the Retreatants

The Facebook stories I shared in the last chapter now bring us back to the story of Catholic media continuing to transform itself and its users' consciousness toward a more participatory sense of faith-based community. Rebranding itself in 2014 from *America Magazine* (a print platform founded by US Jesuits in 1909) to *America Media*, a portal with multiple platforms, *America* in particular has worked to do that on Facebook. On one hand, a steadily growing number of people across the globe engage its page, and constitute most of the Catholic media consumers who participated in the retreat and in the surveys this chapter will now report. On the other hand, they generally come from retired and semi-retired generations of Catholics who bring to social networks an individualist mindset from their passive faith and media habits, leaving room for a deeper shift of consciousness toward unity in diversity. An analysis of survey responses from seventy-four retreatants will show how this Ignatian Facebook retreat helped them to grow qualitatively in relationship with God, each other, and themselves as they conceived a desire to share faith more often on social media in the future.

Recalling the papal quotes on social media in chapter 2, these results affirm the unifying role of charity in effective Catholic online faith-sharing. As Pope Francis has said, charity ensures that online dialogue supports rather than harms interpersonal relations. In his encyclical on ecology, Francis contrasts digital charity with an attitude of egoism:

> Today's media do enable us to communicate and to share our knowledge and affections. Yet at times they also shield us from direct contact with the pain, the fears and the joys of others and the complexity of their personal experiences. For this reason, we should be concerned that, alongside the exciting possibilities offered by these media, a deep and melancholic dissatisfaction with interpersonal relations, or a harmful sense of isolation, can also arise.[135]

In his concern for the impact of digital media on "interpersonal relations," Francis rejects a privatized notion of religion among Catholics who embrace a purely individualist mindset of personal salvation detached from interaction with others. Here Francis suggests an approach that complements the work of digital catechists like Bishop Robert Barron, whose work responds to popular atheism that pushes the "nones" into religious disaffiliation by contrasting the rationality of science with "the irrationality of Catholic faith."[136] Barron's approach is to forge a "new apologetics" to the "nones" by which Catholics can "argue them back" into faith;[137] Francis focuses on grounding spiritual conversations in care for others. Keeping

---

135. Francis, Encyclical Letter *Laudato Si'* [On Care for Our Common Home], May 24, 2015, no. 47, Holy See, http://w2.vatican.va/content/francesco/en/encyclicals/documents/papa-francesco_20150524_enciclica-laudato-si.html.

136. Bishop Robert Barron, *Renewing Our Hope: Essays for the New Evangelization* (Washington, DC: The Catholic University of America Press, 2020), 17.

137. Ibid., 28.

that in mind, this Facebook faith-sharing retreat chose the *Spiritual Exercises* rather than the *Summa Theologica* of St. Thomas Aquinas (Barron's preferred conversational reference point) to accompany Catholics from different generations. The survey data below further illustrates the diversity of existing "Catholic media consumers" who found themselves drawn to this experience.

By implementing a design based upon the concepts outlined in the first two chapters, this online retreat sought to complement the depth of people's offline connections, a goal the survey questions below highlight through their focus on relationality and interaction. Calling for human solidarity amid the coronavirus pandemic, Pope Francis warned again about the dangers of social media interaction fueling egoism. In his 2020 encyclical *Fratelli Tutti,* which was issued halfway into this Facebook group's thirty-day faith-sharing retreat, the pope writes, "Digital communication wants to bring everything out into the open; people's lives are combed over, laid bare and bandied about, often anonymously. Respect for others disintegrates, and even as we dismiss, ignore or keep others distant, we can shamelessly peer into every detail of their lives."[138] Francis underlines here the risks to charity unique to online interaction.

Did the participants of this "Spiritual Exercises Faith-Sharing Retreat Group" disintegrate into this kind of disrespect, adding to the narcissistic isolation of Catholics who hide behind digital anonymity to lash out angrily at each

---

138. Francis, Encyclical Letter *Fratelli Tutti'* [On Fraternity and Social Friendship], Oct. 3, 2020, no. 42, Holy See, http://www.vatican.va/content/francesco/en/encyclicals/documents/papa-francesco_20201003_enciclica-fratelli-tutti.html.

other? The pre-retreat and post-retreat questionnaires, conducted on Survey Monkey and linked to the group page itself for completion, suggest otherwise. Rather than disrespect, they evoke a hopeful story of spiritual growth in charitable relationships, evidenced primarily by retreatants reporting signs of a participatory shift in consciousness toward unity in diversity. To explore this shift, let's compare the pre-retreat survey results to the post-retreat survey responses.

Survey Responses in Their Own Words

Full Survey Monkey charts and written texts from free response questions will be found in appendix 2. To begin the surveys, question 1 asked people beforehand to indicate their intention to participate and afterward to attest they had logged in at least once. Since seventy-four people completed both surveys, this analysis reports only data from those participants, excluding two people who answered "no" to this first question as well as the 138 others who filled out the pre-retreat survey but did not submit the post-retreat survey. The text of the long first question from the pre-retreat survey, explaining the commitment and asking people's intent to participate, as well as of the long first question from the post-retreat survey that asks them to confirm they logged in, can also be found in appendix 2.

The other nineteen questions in each survey give more information about who participated, quantitative data about their habits, and their qualitative interpretation of relational experiences that helped them arrive at new insights, comparing before and after questions in light of trends the research literature on digital media and religious media habits denoted in earlier chapters. This data makes it possible to analyze the findings of both surveys. That analysis in turn will set up chapter 5's broader generational conclusions and suggestions. I linked these anonymous before and after surveys to each other through IP addresses that Survey Monkey recorded. Duplicating questions 2 and 4 on both surveys (regarding their age ranges and religious affiliations) further helped me match participants whose IP addresses varied slightly between surveys. Question 2 on both surveys identified participants' generations using the ranges of birth years that Pew has fixed for them.

▶ Q2: In which generation were you born?

ANSWER CHOICES	RESPONSES	
1901-1927 ("Greatest Generation")	0.00%	0
1928-1945 ("Silent Generation")	8.11%	6
1946-1964 ("Baby Boomers")	50.00%	37
1965-1980 ("Generation X")	24.32%	18
1981-1996 ("Generation Y"/"Millennials")	16.22%	12
1997-2012 ("Generation Z"/"iGeneration")	1.35%	1
TOTAL		74

Exactly half of respondents came from the Baby Boomer generation, a familiar cohort for Catholic ministry and social media. Adding the Silent Generation, just over half (58.11 percent) of retreatants were born before 1965. The next largest groups of participants after Boomers came from Generation X, whose eighteen retreatants represented nearly one in four (24.32 percent) members of the group, and then the sixteen millennials (16.22 percent) of the group. Finally, there was a single member of the iGeneration (1.35 percent) among the seventy-four respondents.

This identical data from question 2 of both surveys reflects what the research of the first two chapters suggested might happen in online Catholic media outreach: Older Catholic media consumers had the strongest faith commitment, interest level, and availability for sticking with a digital retreat lasting thirty days. Younger consumers of Catholic and Ignatian content on Facebook, while willing and interested enough to start the retreat or audit it silently in the larger numbers that chapter 3 reported, could not sustain a commitment for so long. According to design, the group thus became an intentional opportunity for older churchgoing Catholics to form themselves as digital disciples, but in contact with a larger number of younger people than they might normally encounter at Mass. The fact that nearly one in five respondents (17.57 percent) were younger than thirty years old (born after 1980) and four in ten (41.89 percent) of them younger than fifty-six (born after 1964, adding Generation X) allowed for a more age-diverse group than the typical offline parish gathering of semi-retired and retired parishioners.[139] Chapter 5 will address the question of whether people overcame generational differences to have a unified experience and draw further conclusions.

In addition to generational diversity, the digital format of this asynchronous group provided the desired flexibility for people to join from all over the globe, regardless of time zone or culture. Question 3 on the pre-retreat survey indicated that people from four different continents completed it, with almost one in five (17.57 percent) of the seventy-four survey respondents coming from outside the United States. Non-US

---

139. Given the chapter 1 data showing age as the primary demographic area where people's religious habits diverge, this question sets up a key point of generational comparison for other survey questions chapter 5 will revisit.

locations included elsewhere in North America/Central America as well as Asia, Europe, and Australia/ New Zealand.

▶ **Q3:** Where do you live?

ANSWER CHOICES	RESPONSES	
United States of America and territories	82.43%	61
Elsewhere in North America/Central America	6.76%	5
South America	0.00%	0
Europe	4.05%	3
Asia	5.41%	4
Africa	0.00%	0
Australia or New Zealand	1.35%	1
Antarctica	0.00%	0
TOTAL		74

Rather than repeat this geographical inquiry, question 3 on the post-retreat survey asked how often respondents logged on to the group during its four seven-day sessions. Most reported doing so a few times or more each week. For the rest, a small number (nine out of seventy-four) logged on only weekly or less often. This result suggests a fairly strong level of participant engagement and interaction.

▶ **Q3:** On average, how often did you log on to this Facebook faith-sharing group each week?

ANSWER CHOICES	RESPONSES	
More than once a day	9.46%	7
Once a day	29.73%	22
A few times a week	48.65%	36
Weekly	6.76%	5
Less than weekly	5.41%	4
TOTAL		74

With the retreat invitation targeting existing "Catholic media consumers" of *America Media* and other Ignatian Facebook groups, I expected that religious affiliation would be less diverse than the generational and geographic breakdown. That was indeed the case. More than nine in ten participants (91.89 percent) identified as Catholic in question 4. The rest answered Protestant (3), Eastern Orthodox (1), and Other (2). The two "Other" responses came from a departing Catholic seeking to become Baptist (Protestant) and an unaffiliated individual who identified as "Indigenous." The post-retreat survey duplicated this question and got the same results, confirming no change in religious affiliation occurred on the retreat.

▶ **Q4:** How would you describe your current religious affiliation?

ANSWER CHOICES	RESPONSES	
Catholic (including the Eastern Catholic churches)	91.89%	68
Eastern Orthodox Christian	1.35%	1
Protestant (including Anglican Communion)	4.05%	3
Jewish	0.00%	0
Muslim/Islamic	0.00%	0
Nothing in Particular (Atheist, Agnostic, or "None")	0.00%	0
Other (please specify)	2.70%	2
TOTAL		74

Nevertheless, this hoped-for target audience of seventy-four committed Catholics poised to go deeper in digital discipleship was not without its nuances. Reflecting the survey data of the first two chapters, even this predominantly Catholic group reported varying levels of religious identification and observance. Recalling the statistical slide of Catholics through various stages of institutional disaffiliation to self-identification as "nones," a journey in which they gradually feel more connected to God and prayer practices than to institutional religion, pre-survey respondents reported feeling more connected to a Higher Power than to a particular faith community before the retreat. That echoes the finding of earlier chapters that Catholics of all ages risk drifting from communal faith practice into more privatized religiosity (the egoism Pope Francis notes) if digital evangelizers do not challenge them to interact with each other synodally as co-responsible members of a common faith community, rather than as individual consumers of religious content who seek primarily self-satisfaction.

Data from both surveys indicated that respondents did not feel any more connected to this online form of religious community than to a particular community (meaning Catholic for most of them) before the retreat. Indeed, the levels of connection dropped. But the majority of respondents felt at least some connection to the online group, suggesting its power to complement and support offline ties. While only two respondents in question 5 of the pre-retreat survey they felt "no" personal connection to "a particular faith-based community," only three reported feeling "no" connection to this Facebook group on the post-retreat survey.

▶ **Q5:** How strongly do you feel personally connected to a particular faith-based community?

ANSWER CHOICES	RESPONSES	
A lot	71.62%	53
Some	18.92%	14
A little	6.76%	5
Not at all	2.70%	2
TOTAL		74

▶ **Q5:** How strongly did you feel personally connected to this online community during the 30 days of faith-sharing?

ANSWER CHOICES	RESPONSES	
A lot	29.73%	22
Some	41.89%	31
A little	24.32%	18
Not at all	4.05%	3
TOTAL		74

119

Question 6, comparing the self-reported quality of participants' relationships to God before and after the group, further supports this power of online evangelization to complement and enhance the quality of people's offline connections despite the limitations of a digital setting. It suggests digital interaction presented a greater obstacle to respondents connecting with other people in this group than with the invisible God, who remained almost just as accessible to them in personal prayer online as offline. This result evokes the connection-forming power of shared digital prayer—as distinct from mere apologetics—that Christian researchers Keith Anderson and Elizabeth Drescher promote in their work. Whereas almost nine in ten (87.84 percent) participants felt "a lot" of connection to a Higher Power before the retreat, on the post-retreat survey not quite eight in ten (77.03 percent) reported feeling "a lot" of connection to a Higher Power during it.

▶ **Q6:** How strongly do you feel personally connected to a Higher Power as you understand it?

ANSWER CHOICES	RESPONSES	
A lot	87.84%	65
Some	10.81%	8
A little	1.35%	1
Not at all	0.00%	0
TOTAL		74

▶ **Q6:** How strongly did you feel personally connected to a Higher Power as you understand it during the 30 days of faith-sharing?

ANSWER CHOICES	RESPONSES	
A lot	77.03%	57
Some	13.51%	10
A little	9.46%	7
Not at all	0.00%	0
TOTAL		74

Although Questions 5 and 6 hint that some participants felt more connected to God and others outside of this online retreat than in it, the fact that so many people felt connected at all in the Facebook group satisfied this project's modest goal of helping people grow relationally through digital interaction. Previous chapters suggest that the primary challenge for Catholic online evangelization is providing a space for relationality, rather than merely packaged religious content for passive reflection and privatized consumption. Reflecting that insight, question 7 on the pre-retreat survey sought a baseline understanding of participants' faith practices, casting the widest net possible to include online discussion and spiritual reading as "religious events." Even articulated this broadly to cover every possible faith-based activity, both private and communal as well as offline and online, fewer than half of respondents (44.59 percent) reported engaging in a religious activity either offline or online more than once a week before the retreat, and roughly one-third of participants (31.07 percent) reported doing so less than weekly. That means a sizeable number of respondents did not participate at least weekly in religious events, despite their self-identification beforehand as Catholics who felt a strong sense of connection to God. Had the surveys asked just about Sunday Mass or church attendance, these numbers would likely be even lower.

▶ **Q7:** How often have you been involved in a religiously sponsored event (funeral, wedding, church service, online discussion, spiritual reading, prayer or meditation group, etc.) in the past 12 months? Select the response that most closely approximates your attendance.

ANSWER CHOICES	RESPONSES	
None	0.00%	0
1-6 times a year	13.51%	10
7-11 times a year	4.05%	3
Once a month	4.05%	3
2-3 times a month	9.46%	7
Once a week	24.32%	18
More than once a week	44.59%	33
TOTAL		74

Granting the reality that people always feel less connected in social media platforms compared to offline interactions, additional data suggests that even the weakened connections of this online faith-sharing retreat had a strong positive impact on participants' attitudes toward offline religious observance. While this online retreat did not reach any self-declared atheists or agnostics, even the seventy-four retreatants who participated from beginning to end represented (except for the "indigenous" response) Christians in varied stages of affiliation, weighted toward a slightly higher level of participation than the general Catholic population. That provided the mix I sought of fairly active Catholic media consumers who felt more connected to God than to the faith community, leaving room to grow in the latter bond. Retreatants from many generations, not all equally observant, grew together in a desire for interpersonal connection.

In perhaps the most significant finding of these surveys, respondents reported an intention to move toward greater religious practice after the retreat than before it. Question 7 on the post-retreat survey asked about their plans moving forward to engage in religious practices, construed in the same broad way as this question on the pre-retreat survey. Twenty-five of the respondents (34.25 percent) who answered this question, more than one-third of the group, said they planned to do so "more often." The majority of respondents, 65.5 percent, said "about the same." Nobody said "less often" and one retreatant skipped the question.

▶ **Q7:** How often do you intend to attend a religiously sponsored event (funeral, wedding, church service, online discussion, spiritual reading, prayer or meditation group, etc.) moving forward from this faith-sharing group into the future?"

ANSWER CHOICES	RESPONSES	
More often than I did before this faith-sharing group	34.25%	25
About the same as I always do	65.75%	48
Less often than I did before the group	0.00%	0
I don't plan to attend religious services in the future	0.00%	0
TOTAL		73

Even though this retreat could not prove a causal relationship between online faith-sharing and offline attendance at church events, the fact that more than one-third of survey respondents left with a resolution to participate in religious activities "more often" conforms to the statistical correlation between online habits and offline behavior that the social media research of chapter 1 reported. So does the fact that nobody left the retreat less inclined toward offline religious participation. The shift that occurred for these survey respondents in an explicitly Catholic digital community, as opposed to the secular online groups described in chapter 1, will set up some hopeful conclusions and recommendations in chapter 5.

The next questions clarify participants' digital media background and habits, showing promising signs of growth in digital fluency through the online faith-sharing retreat. Question 8 on the pre-retreat survey asked about the importance of online interaction in their lives before the retreat. As expected in a group of experienced social media users invited exclusively from existing Facebook groups rather than recruited offline, more than half (52.7 percent) said "important," with another large fraction of retreatants (21.62 percent) saying "highly important." Nevertheless, a sizeable number of participants landed somewhere in the middle on this question, with the second largest segment (22.97 percent) saying "neutral." These results indicated that room existed for participants' consciousness to shift on this issue during the retreat as they grew more comfortable with participatory digital interaction.

▶ **Q8:** How important is online interaction (e.g., Instagram, Facebook, comment boxes, other social media platforms) in your life?

ANSWER CHOICES	RESPONSES	
Highly Important	21.62%	16
Important	52.70%	39
Neutral	22.97%	17
Unimportant	2.70%	2
Highly Unimportant	0.00%	0
TOTAL		74

In another promising result, on question 8 of the post-retreat survey these same participants reported higher levels of satisfaction with this particular use of Facebook than the importance they afforded to digital communication in general beforehand. Whereas relatively few (21.62 percent) of these Facebook-using respondents described online interaction as "highly important" to their lives before the retreat, more than one third (36.49 percent) described as "highly satisfactory" the use of Facebook to facilitate this thirty-day faith-sharing group. Although five retreatants found the use of Facebook "unsatisfactory," slightly higher than the two who described social media as "unimportant" to their lives before the retreat, a larger movement toward satisfaction with online interaction in this particular group appeared on the post-retreat survey. Compare question 8 on the post-retreat survey in the following table with question 8 on the pre-retreat table of results above.

▶ **Q8:** This online retreat utilized Facebook. How satisfied do you feel about the use of Facebook to facilitate the group interactions?

ANSWER CHOICES	RESPONSES	
Highly Satisfactory	36.49%	27
Satisfactory	36.49%	27
Neutral	20.27%	15
Unsatisfactory	6.76%	5
Highly Unsatisfactory	0.00%	0
TOTAL		74

Looking next at more specifically religious experiences of digital media, question 9 on the pre-retreat survey asked about retreatants' frequency of using it for faith-sharing. An equal number of pre-retreat survey respondents (74.98 percent total) said "a lot" and "some," but relatively few (21.61 percent) said "a little" even fewer (5.41 percent) said "not at all," indicating that more than one quarter of participants had little to no experience sharing their faith online. This result left room for this Facebook retreat to help members grow more comfortable discussing their religious experiences on social media, addressing the relative failure of Catholic online media to do so.

▶ **Q9:** How much, if at all, have you shared your faith with others online during your life?

ANSWER CHOICES	RESPONSES	
A lot	36.49%	27
Some	36.49%	27
A little	21.62%	16
Not at all	5.41%	4
TOTAL		74

Once more reflecting the power of apparently limited digital relationships to influence people's social habits, question 9 of the post-retreat survey asked how often these same participants intended to discuss faith-based content online moving forward from this Facebook retreat experience. A sizeable number (39.19 percent—29 people) said they intended to do so "more often," while yet more (59.46 percent—44 people) said "about the same" and just one person (1.35 percent) said "less often." Overall this comparison implies that while this group's members had some experience sharing their faith online before the Facebook faith-sharing retreat, their interactions in it had a noticeably positive impact on their resolve to do so in the future.

▶ **Q9:** How likely are you to discuss faith-based content with others online as you move forward from this faith-sharing group into the future?

ANSWER CHOICES	RESPONSES	
More often than I did before this faith-sharing group	39.19%	29
About the same as I always do	59.46%	44
Less often than I did before the group	1.35%	1
I don't plan to share my faith online in the future	0.00%	0
TOTAL		74

As noted in chapter 1, researcher Nancy Baym found that online interaction influences offline habits in secular communities, and this retreat suggests that this influence might be true of faith-based communities as well. Question 10 on the surveys offered some particularly relevant data. Unsurprisingly for a group that skewed older, participants claimed a deeper experience of faith-sharing offline than online, with more than half of respondents (54.05 percent) saying they had "a lot" of it on question 10 of the pre-retreat survey compared to the less than half (39.19 percent) who said the same of online faith-sharing in question 9.

▶ **Q10:** How much, if at all, have you shared your faith with others offline (face-to-face) during your life?

ANSWER CHOICES	RESPONSES	
A lot	54.05%	40
Some	37.84%	28
A little	8.11%	6
Not at all	0.00%	0
TOTAL		74

Bearing in mind the positive correlation between online and offline social habits, comparing this result to question 10 on the post-retreat survey suggests yet another positive impact. Even though retreatants began the online group with more faith-sharing experience offline than online, question 10 on the post-retreat survey showed the retreat having a slightly greater influence on their faith-sharing habits offline than online. Whereas almost four in ten (39.19 percent) said in question 9 of the post-retreat survey they intended to share faith online "more often" in the future, three more people (43.24) said in question 10 they intended to do so offline "more often" in the future. No respondents intended to discuss faith offline "less often" and more than a half (56.76 percent) intended to do so "about the same." Considering the greater efficacy of offline evangelization than online outreach, it seems significant that participating in online faith-sharing may have increased respondents' confidence about sharing faith offline.

▶ **Q10:** How likely are you to discuss faith-based content with others offline (face-to-face) moving forward from this online faith-sharing group?

ANSWER CHOICES	RESPONSES	
More often than I did before this faith-sharing group	43.24%	32
About the same as I always do	56.76%	42
Less often than I did before the group	0.00%	0
I don't plan to share my faith offline in the future	0.00%	0
TOTAL		74

These results imply that a large number of respondents left the retreat with greater zeal for engaging others in both online and offline spiritual conversation. But what about their relationship to themselves as manifested in their desires for self-growth? In free response format, question 11 on the surveys asked participants to share what they wanted for themselves before the retreat and what they believed afterwards they actually received on it. As guides of the *Spiritual Exercises* know from experience, retreatants often receive a different grace from what they expected beforehand, signifying that they did not attempt to control or steer the prayer in predetermined directions. This discrepancy usually denotes authentic spiritual growth in one's relationships to God, others, and oneself, insofar as real change often occurs somewhere in this shift of consciousness from expectation to experience. While question 11 on both surveys offered a free response format, with the full texts of individual responses available in appendix 2 to save space here, Survey Monkey provides a word cloud feature to illustrate the key themes in retreatants' responses by ranking the most commonly used words visually by font size from largest to smallest. The question 11 cloud in the pre-retreat survey appears as follows.

▶ **Q11:** What particular hopes or desires do you bring to this online faith-sharing experience? Please write them in the space below.

will deepen relationship God spiritual continue growing closer God hope grow learn structure love become community develop understand online share relationship God God welcome others spirituality faith deepen faith life grow hope journey experience interesting better idea time new feel prayer life group grow closer God help pray

Seventy-two participants answered this free response question and two skipped it. The next most common words in descending frequency were "others," "life, "share," "hope," "God," and "experience." Other phrases like "grow closer God" and "relationship God" appear smaller here but may be lumped in with their larger cousins such as "God" and "faith" as relating to their personal connection with God. Grouped together, they reflect the reality seen in appendix 2 that most responses to this question expressed privatized religious desires for more faith for themselves and connection to God. That may seem ironic since they indicated on questions 5 and 6 that they already felt significantly more connected to God than to the Catholic Church (to which sixty-eight of the seventy-four belong) before the retreat. A sizeable minority nevertheless expressed other-centered desires for deeper connections with others.

In light of these graces that they sought, what graces did participants actually receive in the online faith-sharing retreat? Signifying an authentic experience of spiritual growth through interaction with the prayer material and with each other, as opposed to what Lonergan might call an inauthentic experience of participants scripting God's role in their prayer within the cognitive biases of their isolated minds, the word cloud for question 11 on the post-retreat survey differed from the pre-retreat survey. This word cloud for question 11 of the post-retreat survey, again answered by seventy-two people and skipped by two, appears as follows.

▶ **Q11:** What particular hopes or desires did you find were fulfilled in the experience? Please write them in the space below.

learning connection God also strengthen Jesus Deepening love practicing able connected faith closer God prayer Lord helped connection hoped spiritual exercises experience relationship God God grow retreat Ignatian Spirituality life way wanted deeper found prayer life understanding God s better hope feel time day helpful community desires fulfilled exercises Learn St Ignatius desire spiritual

Visually, this post-retreat word cloud's enlargement over the pre-retreat cloud suggests an expansion of spiritual vocabulary, with a higher level of critical thinking (an ingredient of success in online group formation, as chapter 3 noted) appearing as a fruit of self-knowledge gained on the retreat. Note that interpersonal words like "help," "love," and "understand(ing)" appear larger after the retreat than before, being used more often, and suggest respondents received more of these graces than they had asked for. The ranking and list of most common words here also differs from the pre-retreat cloud. The most commonly used word this time was "retreat," even though it did not appear in the pre-retreat word cloud at all. That must reflect at least in part the expanded vocabulary the *Exercises* gave respondents to talk about their religious experiences, considering that the Ignatian material uses the word "retreat" often. But it also reflects the reality, seen in appendix 2, of some participants who wrote that they discovered this Facebook group to be a true restful and restorative experience of being on retreat in a way they had not anticipated. This overall expansion of vocabulary and notable addition of a previously unused word ("retreat") to the top of the post-retreat list suggests a shift (or what Lonergan might call a conversion) of consciousness among respondents toward a more community-centered mindset.

Question 12 on the pre-retreat survey asked how often it occurred to participants to discuss their faith on Facebook before the retreat, narrowing the scope of question 9 to the particular social media platform this retreat adopted. It showed participants less inclined to discuss faith on Facebook than online in general. Whereas almost four in ten (36.19 percent) respondents to question 9 said they discussed faith online "a lot" before the retreat, fewer one in ten (6.76 percent) respondents to question 12 said it "always" occurred to them to do so on Facebook (and only 22.97 percent said "usually") before the retreat.

▶ **Q12:** How often, if ever, does it occur to you to discuss faith-based content on Facebook?

ANSWER CHOICES	RESPONSES	
Always	6.76%	5
Usually	22.97%	17
Sometimes	41.89%	31
Rarely	18.92%	14
Never	9.46%	7
TOTAL		74

As I tried to determine the best way to run this Ignatian faith-sharing group, I looked back at their experience of Facebook. Almost four in ten (36.49 percent) participants had reported that they found it "highly satisfactory" on question 8. Question 12 on the post-retreat survey asked them for free response feedback on any other social media platforms they might suggest for online faith-sharing in the future. Aware that a non-response would be recorded as "no suggestion," fifty-eight retreatants answered this free response question and eighteen skipped it, indicating general satisfaction with Facebook. The following word cloud summarizes the key words in their responses to the question.

▶ **Q12:** Other than Facebook, is there another digital media format you would suggest that America use for an online faith-sharing group? Please write your suggestion in the blank. If you do not write anything, your answer will be recorded as "no suggestion."

use website might retreat present found group social media worked meeting Facebook community Zoom comments suggestion Instagram people Twitter well need know Microsoft Teams Maybe Youtube

The size of these fonts again illustrates the most common word in descending frequency of use in the written responses that appendix 2 reprints in full. Sixteen participants mentioned "Zoom," a highly participatory technology that might have been a viable option for this group had it been mentioned in any of the social media literature or widely available during the design phase of the retreat that occurred long before Covid-19 made it a household name. Another ten responses mentioned

"Facebook," primarily in the context of expressing their approval of it with some minor quibbles. The next most common words "suggestion," "worked," and "well" proved incidental in mostly positive reports about Facebook. A smaller number of people mentioned YouTube, Microsoft Teams, Instagram, or a website as possible platforms. This result confirmed that most respondents felt satisfied with Facebook as the best format for this group at the time, although a minority showed interest in trying the emerging Zoom platform too.

Question 13 on both surveys repeated a question from researcher John Dyer, cited in chapter 1, about whether people consider online community a form of real community. It sought to see if the retreatants reflected his findings and whether the experience of this online faith-sharing group changed any of their minds about it. On the pre-retreat survey, more than half (55.41 percent) considered online community to be real, with the next highest segment (37.84 percent) unsure and only a few (6.76 percent) saying no.

▶ **Q13:** Do you consider online community to be a type of "real" community?

ANSWER CHOICES	RESPONSES	
Yes	55.41%	41
No	6.76%	5
Unsure	37.84%	28
TOTAL		74

Question 13 on the post-retreat survey showed six folks moving out of the "unsure" response in both directions, with two more retreatants saying "yes" and four more saying "no" when asked about their experience of this Facebook group specifically. Reinforcing the role of discernment in helping reduce a faith-based group to its committed core of potential disciples, this data demonstrates that this Facebook space did help a small number of participants clarify their opinions of its ability to form "real" community. Even though six out of twenty-eight "unsure" responses moving their position remains statistically insignificant, and perhaps underlines the limits of Facebook as a digital bulletin board to settle this question definitively, it did reveal one helpful result. From an evangelization standpoint, the two people who moved into the "yes" response in the following post-retreat data will be two more digital disciples likely to use Facebook as a place to establish a sense of real connection with faith groups. Also, as the next chapter will revisit in its conclusions about these results, younger participants moved from "unsure" to "yes" and older participants moved to "no," perhaps revealing a lingering hint of the generational disconnect on this issue that Dyer found in 2011.

▶ **Q13:** Do you consider this Facebook faith-sharing group to have been a type of "real" community?

ANSWER CHOICES	RESPONSES	
Yes	58.11%	43
No	12.16%	9
Unsure	29.73%	22
TOTAL		74

Returning to the difference between the graces sought and the graces received, question 14 asked retreatants in a "choose all" response to identify with outcomes commonly experienced by people making the *Exercises* offline. These outcomes addressed their relationships with God, themselves, and others. The pre-retreat version of this question shows, in descending percentages of respondents who selected each one, that retreatants desired a better relationship with God, more knowledge about Ignatian spirituality, a stronger connection to a faith-based community, more knowledge about Catholic teachings, "other," and "unsure."

▶ **Q14:** What outcome would you like to see from this online faith-sharing group? Please choose all that apply

ANSWER CHOICES	RESPONSES	
A better relationship with God	82.43%	61
Stronger sense of connection to a faith-based community	66.22%	49
More knowledge about Catholic teachings	47.30%	35
More knowledge about Ignatian spirituality	74.32%	55
Unsure	1.35%	1
Other (please specify)	4.05%	3
Total Respondents: 74		

Before the retreat, these participants prioritized their relationships with God and self (insofar as knowledge represents a form of self-relationship) over their relationship with others in a faith-based community as desired outcomes of this online faith-sharing group. That may seem strange given that many of them, before the retreat, reported already having a stronger connection to God and to self (in their self-identification as Catholic) than to a particular faith-based community and to an active sense of religious observance before the retreat. Recalling Christian Smith's data cited in chapter 1, it may simply reflect some of the institutional distrust among Boomers as well as among younger generations.

In a hopeful sign, question 14 on the post-retreat survey reported a change in these relational priorities. Here the percentage of respondents seeking a better relationship with God dropped from just over eight in ten (82.42 percent) seeking it before the retreat to just under seven in ten (68.49 percent) who said afterward they received it. Paradoxically, the retreat experience also changed the way they prioritized its outcomes: Instead of only the percentages shifting while the order of priorities remained, question 14 showed a shift of focus away from the outcome of a better relationship with God before the retreat to the outcome of growing in knowledge of Ignatian spirituality after it.

▶ **Q14:** What outcomes did you see in your spiritual life at the end of this online faith-sharing group? Please choose all that apply

ANSWER CHOICES	RESPONSES	
A better relationship with God	68.49%	50
Stronger sense of connection to a faith-based community	28.77%	21
More knowledge about Catholic teachings	30.14%	22
More knowledge about Ignatian spirituality	91.78%	67
Unsure	5.48%	4
Other (please specify)	16.44%	12
Total Respondents: 73		

Unlike the pre-retreat survey's version of this question, the order of most commonly selected outcomes on this post-retreat inventory of received graces turned out to be more knowledge about Ignatian spirituality, a better relationship with God, more knowledge about Catholic teachings, a stronger sense of connection to a faith-based community, "other," and "unsure." This result affirms the usefulness of Facebook for building shared knowledge about Ignatian prayer methods in a way that bolsters rather than fragments interpersonal connections with God and others. They also imply that "Ignatian spirituality" proved to be a significant benefit as well as draw for the retreat, recalling the demographic of the group which took part: older, mostly active, American Catholics seeking the *Exercises*.

All three interconnected relationships of spirituality (God, others, and self) seemed to find support in the spiritual conversations of this Facebook retreat. Far from stifling real connection as Pope Francis warns happens too often on social media detached from any context of Christian charity, online faith-sharing supports these relationships by fostering interaction. Supporting this link, question 15 on the pre-retreat survey revealed that the majority of retreatants' online relationships also figured in their offline lives, recalling the power of shared knowledge formation on social media to inspire additional growth outside of it.

▶ **Q15:** How many of the people you know online also play a role in your offline life outside of the internet?

ANSWER CHOICES	RESPONSES	
A lot	29.73%	22
Some	45.95%	34
A few	18.92%	14
None at all	5.41%	4
TOTAL		74

Question 15 on the post-retreat survey amended this inquiry to examine respondents' interest in participating in more such groups at *America*'s Facebook page. More than eight in ten participants said "yes." Most of the rest reported feeling "unsure," with only one person saying "no." This result attests to the generally positive nature of their retreat experience, as chapter 3 narrated anecdotally in their own words.

▶ **Q15:** Based on this experience, would you be interested in participating in another online faith-sharing group at the America Media Facebook page?

ANSWER CHOICES	RESPONSES	
Yes	82.19%	60
No	1.37%	1
Unsure	16.44%	12
TOTAL		73

Exploring how this group impacted the participants' attitudes regarding their digital relationships, question 16 indicated that they grew more comfortable sharing their faith and personal experiences (as opposed to exchanging opinions) online throughout the thirty-day retreat. Their responses established another baseline to measure growth in participatory interaction from before to after the retreat. In this question on the pre-retreat survey, only one in three (33.78 percent) reported feeling "a lot" of comfort sharing their faith with others online before starting the retreat.

▶ **Q16:** How comfortable do you feel with talking about your personal faith and religious experiences, as opposed to exchanging opinions, in an online faith-sharing group?

ANSWER CHOICES	RESPONSES	
A lot	33.78%	25
Some	44.59%	33
A little	21.62%	16
Not at all	0.00%	0
TOTAL		74

For comparison, question 16 of the post-retreat survey asked more specifically about how comfortable participants felt sharing their faith in this Facebook group. This time, just over four in ten (45.95 percent) said "a lot," a gain of nine people over the pre-retreat survey that satisfied a major desire of this retreat to help participants grow in an area where chapter 1 reported Catholics traditionally lag. Compare the following table to the last one.

▶ **Q16:** How comfortable did you feel talking about your personal faith and religious experiences, as opposed to exchanging opinions, in this Facebook group?

ANSWER CHOICES	RESPONSES	
A lot	45.95%	34
Some	33.78%	25
A little	14.86%	11
Not at all	5.41%	4
TOTAL		74

Finally, the last four questions on each survey explored the particular graces of the four weeks of the *Spiritual Exercises*, inspecting the quality of respondents' faith-sharing experiences of these themes. Question 17 asked about the first week grace of knowing themselves as loved sinners, the starting point of the *Exercises* for St. Ignatius. On the pre-retreat survey, almost seven in ten participants (69.86 percent) "very much" sensed this grace in their spiritual lives before the retreat.

▶ **Q17:** To what extent does this statement accurately describe your spiritual life? Statement: "I have a deeply felt sense of God's love for me even though I am a sinner."

ANSWER CHOICES	RESPONSES	
Very Much	69.86%	51
Somewhat	24.66%	18
Not Much	4.11%	3
Not At All	0.00%	0
Unsure	1.37%	1
TOTAL		73

On question 17 of the post-retreat survey, the number of people saying they received this grace during the first week of the online faith-sharing retreat dropped to 50 percent. This comparison offers another reminder that online interaction never matches the depth of offline interaction. It also illuminates once more the paradox that while many participants entered the retreat seeking to grow in the areas where they already felt the strongest connection (i.e., their relationship with God), the actual growth occurred in areas of weakness (i.e., knowledge of Ignatian spirituality) they had not foreseen.

▶ **Q17:** To what extent does this statement accurately describe the grace you received in Week One of the retreat? Statement: "I grew in a deeply felt sense of God's love for me even though I am a sinner."

ANSWER CHOICES	RESPONSES	
Very Much	50.00%	37
Somewhat	32.43%	24
Not Much	8.11%	6
Not At All	4.05%	3
Unsure	5.41%	4
TOTAL		74

Question 18 focused on the second week grace of desiring to follow Jesus, revealing stronger numbers than any other week. About three-quarters of participants (74.32 percent) "very much" felt this desire entering the group, far more than said they felt God's love for them in spite of their sinfulness. Added to the smaller number (22.97 percent) of respondents who answered "somewhat," a fairly positive image emerges of how participants viewed their sense of following Jesus.

▶ **Q18:** To what extent does this statement accurately describe your spiritual life? Statement: "I feel a desire to accompany Jesus and labor with him in his ongoing ministry."

ANSWER CHOICES	RESPONSES	
Very Much	74.32%	55
Somewhat	22.97%	17
Not Much	2.70%	2
Not At All	0.00%	0
Unsure	0.00%	0
TOTAL		74

In question 18 of the post-retreat survey, this number shifted. A bit over half of retreatants (51.35 percent) "very much" and a bit over a third (36.49 percent) "somewhat" experienced this desire during the faith-sharing group itself.

Within the context of Ignatian spiritual practice, these numbers may suggest a move toward greater self-knowledge of one's own limits in relation to God, insofar as it suggests that people ended the retreat with a more realistic sense of their capacity for spiritual growth after encountering the challenging reflections of Ignatius. It may also denote again that retreatants grew more in unexpected areas and less in areas where they already felt strong before the retreat. As chapter 5 will conclude, retreatants experienced this growth together as they moved from diverse ages and perspectives into a shared understanding.

▶ **Q18:** To what extent does this statement accurately describe the grace you received in Week Two of the retreat? Statement: "I grew in my desire to accompany Jesus and labor with him in his ongoing ministry."

ANSWER CHOICES	RESPONSES	
Very Much	51.35%	38
Somewhat	36.49%	27
Not Much	2.70%	2
Not At All	0.00%	0
Unsure	9.46%	7
TOTAL		74

In question 19 on the Week Three grace of suffering with Jesus in his passion, the largest increase in "very much" responses of any week occurred from before to after the retreat. Additionally, the smallest number of people reported experiencing this grace both before and after the retreat out of any week in the *Exercises,* highlighting it as a particular area of potential growth for this group. From an Ignatian perspective, that appears especially significant because of the lived experience that people bond together more closely when they share sufferings than when they share joyful moments. Only a small number (16.22 percent of retreatants) said this third week grace "very much" described their spiritual life before the retreat.

▶ **Q19**: To what extent does this statement accurately describe your spiritual life? Statement: "I feel like I have suffered with Jesus on the cross."

ANSWER CHOICES	RESPONSES	
Very Much	16.22%	12
Somewhat	54.05%	40
Not Much	17.57%	13
Not At All	9.46%	7
Unsure	2.70%	2
TOTAL		74

On question 19 of the post-retreat survey, almost one in three retreatants (32.43 percent) reported experiencing a desire "very much" to suffer with Jesus during the retreat, twice the number of people who reported having done so before it started. This third week grace carries particular importance in the context of the Exercises, insofar as inexperienced retreatants find it easier to follow Jesus in his public ministry during Week Two than they do in his suffering. While the number of participants who identified strongly with the graces of the first two weeks dropped from before to after the retreat, the opposite happened with this third week grace, suggesting this retreat helped them get in touch with their sufferings more deeply and bring them to the cross.

▶ **Q19:** To what extent does this statement accurately describe the grace you received in Week Three of the retreat? Statement: "I experienced a stronger desire to suffer with Jesus on the cross."

ANSWER CHOICES	RESPONSES	
Very Much	32.43%	24
Somewhat	37.84%	28
Not Much	9.46%	7
Not At All	6.76%	5
Unsure	13.51%	10
TOTAL		74

In Ignatian spirituality, this ability to suffer with Jesus compassionately reflects an essential foundation of interpersonal connection grounded in the ability to feel loved by him despite one's flaws and the ability to follow him when things go well. It evokes the Christian teaching that one must first suffer with Jesus in order to fully experience the joy of his resurrection, the subject of question 20 on the fourth week grace of rejoicing in the resurrection. Despite relatively few participants (16.22 percent) entering the retreat saying they "very much" had suffered with Jesus, over half (51.35) percent entered it reporting that they had "very much" rejoiced with the risen Lord in gratitude for his gifts, suggesting less room for growth in the latter grace.

▶ **Q20:** To what extent does this statement accurately describe your spiritual life? Statement: "I feel like I have rejoiced with the risen Lord, Jesus Christ, in gratitude for all he gives me."

ANSWER CHOICES	RESPONSES	
Very Much	51.35%	38
Somewhat	36.49%	27
Not Much	10.81%	8
Not At All	0.00%	0
Unsure	1.35%	1
TOTAL		74

Half of the respondents (51.35 percent) also said they "very much" rejoiced more deeply with the risen Jesus during the retreat itself. Meanwhile, the number reporting "unsure" on the post-retreat survey rose as "somewhat" and "not much" fell. One possible explanation, based on Facebook analytics of comments by participants provided in appendix C, could be that due to outside commitments some of the seventy-four post-survey respondents struggled to keep up with the daily posts in the final week. Another explanation might be the common observation among Ignatian spiritual directors that retreatants who experience suffering deeply in the Third Week of the *Exercises,* as many on this retreat did, may ask for a little more time to sit with their current struggles alongside the suffering Jesus before switching gears to joy. Some here did.

▶ **Q20:** To what extent does this statement accurately describe the grace you received in Week Four of the retreat? Statement: "I rejoiced more deeply with the risen Lord, Jesus Christ, in gratitude for all he gives me."

ANSWER CHOICES	RESPONSES	
Very Much	51.35%	38
Somewhat	25.68%	19
Not Much	5.41%	4
Not At All	1.35%	1
Unsure	16.22%	12
TOTAL		74

Conclusion: Catholic Media in a Digital Age

Online interaction, while not as impactful as face-to-face interaction, can be beneficial in motivating great zeal for both offline and online evangelization. Secular and theological insights, applied to this experience, suggest that online faith-sharing can build on and feed back into offline religious community. Healthy Christian community can flow into and out of online interactions in a participatory way that strengthens existing faith bonds through a unifying exchange that digital media makes possible.

Writing to the Corinthians, Paul reminded them of the power of charity: "Love is patient, love is kind. It is not jealous, [love] is not pompous, it is not inflated, it is not rude, it does not seek its own interests, it is not quick-tempered, it does not brood over injury, it does not rejoice over wrongdoing but rejoices with the truth. It bears all things, believes all things, hopes all things, endures all things. Love never fails."[140] Rooted in this selfless spirit, participants in this retreat grew in a healthy awareness of participatory connection to God and each other in a virtual community. Chapter 5 will summarize their intergenerational experience of this thirty-day retreat group and draw some tentative conclusions and recommendations for the future.

---

140. 1 Cor 13:4-8 (New American Bible Revised Edition).

Chapter 5

A Handbook for Digital Evangelization

Our story now draws to a close with some big-picture observations and suggestions. My general purpose in the online retreat was to evangelize Catholic media consumers through social media; more specifically, through a thirty-day online faith-sharing retreat group based on the *Spiritual Exercises of St. Ignatius*. This broad goal succeeded, aided by the choice of an asynchronous design as a reasonable compromise between competing values. Participants entered generously into the experience of an online faith-sharing group using social media to form a community across different generations which do not normally interact.

Our retreat succeeded at increasing their comfort with sharing faith online and offline. It also succeeded at boosting the intention, especially among younger members, to participate more often in sacred activities. The value of their online sharing manifested itself in the shift from expectations to results. Retreatants did achieve the specific goals and outcomes for the four weeklong sessions centered on the *Exercises'* prescribed graces of choosing to accept oneself as a sinner loved by God, to follow Jesus, to suffer with Jesus, and to rejoice with Jesus. They succeeded even more in receiving the unexpected graces of bringing their sufferings to God and growing closer to one another. These results suggest necessary modifications to how members might be recruited to this kind of group and how their hopes might be defined, so as to form an online community that reaches beyond a familiar bubble of believers.

What Participants Gained

The stories and survey responses in chapter 4 showed that online faith-sharing in this Facebook group encouraged and strengthened the seventy-four respondents' offline relationships without replacing them. As the secular research literature surveyed in chapter 1 hinted could occur, most members reported achieving some level of connection (to God, themselves, and others) through the thirty-day faith-sharing format that moved them beyond privatized consumption of multimedia content into a participatory interchange about their prayer experiences. A substantial number intended to share their faith online and especially offline more often after the retreat. This implies the "Spiritual Exercises Faith-Sharing Retreat Group" was modestly successful in achieving its general goals, objectives, and expected outcomes for evangelizing Catholic media consumers by digitally enabling their spiritual growth, particularly in interpersonal relationships among those who completed the retreat and surveys. Those seventy-four respondents indicated that they gained knowledge of Ignatian spirituality and grew in digital discipleship as they shifted their consciousness of an "online retreat" from passive reflection on videos to a participatory use of digital media for spiritual conversation.

First, the retreat sought to form online interactive religious groups of various generations. Appendix D, summarizing key survey responses by age, documents the group's basic success at uniting people from a full range of generations in a group faith-sharing experience. No sharp divisions emerged to suggest a clash among generations, even though too few millennial respondents participated to draw firm conclusions about their experience with other generations, and other generations with them. The fact that the different generations did not conflict—nor were there any violations of Facebook community guidelines—demonstrates that Catholics from a variety of generations can engage charitably in positive, respectful, and affirming conversation through a Facebook group. This unity amid diversity, illustrated with anecdotes in chapter 3 and confirmed by survey data in chapter 4, supports my general goal to unite people in a common experience that fostered spiritual growth in a digital context.

Second, the retreat demonstrated that a month-long commitment to explore and deepen faith on social media is challenging but possible. The seventy-four survey respondents fulfilled some clear goals of evangelization as presented in chapter 2 growth in articulation of faith, in their desire to share faith online, and in their desire to share faith offline. The pre-retreat and post-retreat surveys showed the promise of an online faith-sharing group to address the significant pastoral need for Catholics to grow more comfortable at sharing their faith. In particular, it is noteworthy that retreatants felt that they were participating online in a real interpersonal community. Pre-digital Catholic media tended to present prepackaged content in a sender-receiver fashion, whereas this Facebook group invited participants into a many-to-many interchange.

Third, these results address several of the vital issues I pointed out in chapters 1, 2, and 3. Chapter 1 outlined the digital shift from packaged to participatory media communication according to the philosophy of Marshall McLuhan, of secular research literature on the youth-oriented culture of digital media, and of research on the recent breakdown in transmitting Catholicism to younger generations. These insights account for the pastoral problem that arises because Catholics do not manage to share their faith effectively online. This Facebook retreat offers a sound framework to address this challenge and to study the results.

Chapter 2 provided a theological basis for the retreat by examining *communio,* the Trinitarian model of unity-in-diversity for Christian community since apostolic times. Pope Francis has invited the Catholic Church to practice that model with a synodal spirit of openness at all levels of social communication. Reflecting the New Evangelization's call to discern fresh methods for sharing the good news in secularized contexts, the retreat sought to help participants shift from packaged to participatory ecclesial dialogue. Chapter 2 then showed how the *Spiritual Exercises,* as well as the Ignatian leadership principles Francis learned from them and from his experience of Jesuit governance, provided me models I could use as the moderator of this online faith-sharing group to craft a productive social media environment for evangelizing interchange. The satisfaction that most of the seventy-four respondents reported about the Facebook format indicates that the group's interactive format helped promote more meaningful participation through the addition of a faith-sharing dimension, something that is often missing from Catholic online retreats.

Chapter 3 described the design and implementation of the retreat according to the principle of *communio,* employing faith-based media according to secular best practices for the formation of online community. It then suggested key elements of Bernard J.F. Lonergan's theological method as a pastoral framework for this retreat to encourage a participatory shift in consciousness, setting up religious conversion to deeper faith in God as a possible outcome. Applying Lonergan's method proved partially successful, insofar as participants seemed to experience an authentic shift of consciousness from individuality to community. Rather than primarily seeking to boost retreatants' personal sense of connection to a higher power, through the faith-sharing dialogue I sought to move them from privatized to more communal attitudes about their use of Catholic media, and so this shift fulfilled a key aspiration.

Before I draw some conclusions about the limits of these successes and suggest additional adjustments if such a Facebook group were to be used in the future, I will break down key survey data by generation, showing that the seventy-four survey respondents achieved a noticeable degree of unity across all age cohorts. This data appears in appendix D. A few examples show how participants, even in this small sample size, started out in ways that reflected the age-based divisions as pointed out in research literature to be common with Catholics and digital media, but moved in encouraging new directions. Specifically, these examples suggest the group's successful intergenerational unity as revealed in a feeling of connection to the Facebook group, a desire to share faith more often in the future, and a sense of online community as real community.

In terms of generational attitudes toward faith, the pre-retreat survey revealed that younger generations do not evince religious behaviors the way older generations did and do. For example, those claiming "a lot" of connection to a faith community declined steadily from the Silent Generation to the Millennials, as data in chapters 1 and 2 on religious disaffiliation suggested it might. Millennials reported a low sense of connection with their faith community (meaning the

Catholic Church for all twelve of them) and those who felt the least connection before the retreat.

However, the post-retreat survey showed generational attitudes shifting over the thirty-day experience in ways that broke up these age-based trends somewhat. Among all age cohorts, Baby Boomers reported the largest percentage who felt "a lot" of connection to the Facebook faith-sharing group, followed by the Silent Generation and Generation X respectively. Most of the millennials also felt some level of connection, although they struggled more than the Boomers to log in regularly during the retreat. This suggests Boomer respondents were more adept in using the digital format of this group to feel connected to the Catholic community.

Building on this movement, question 9 showed all generations of those who completed the retreat and surveys reporting comparable growth in their desire to engage online faith-sharing. While millennials were the most likely on the pre-retreat survey to say they had "a lot" of experience with it, roughly the same percentage of each generation (excepting the sole Generation Z participant who completed the surveys) indicated on the post-retreat survey an intention to share faith online "more often" afterwards. Comparing this question's results from both surveys indicates that diverse respondents generally arrived at the same resolution regarding future online faith-sharing.

Question 10 gave similar hints of unity arising from diverse starting points. Whereas younger participants had been the most likely to have online faith-sharing experience before the retreat, question 10 on the pre-retreat survey found older participants most likely to claim "a lot" of experience with offline faith-sharing beforehand. On the post-retreat survey, however, question 10 showed a comparable rise in the percentages of Boomers, Generation X, and millennials intending to share their faith offline "more often" in the future. These responses indicate that members of all ages grew at about the same rate in their desires to share faith offline as well as online.

The above results show group members of all ages growing more comfortable about sharing their faith with others. Additional survey data support this conclusion. Question 12 on the pre-retreat survey indicates that most respondents of all age cohorts shared a tendency to think of Facebook only "sometimes" as a venue for faith-sharing before the retreat. Recalling the indication of question 9 that many respondents left the retreat more resolved to share their faith online in the future, a shift toward greater openness about using social media for spiritual conversation seems apparent.

Repeating the question of researcher John Dyer in chapter 1 about whether online community constitutes real community, question 13 sought to find if older generations of respondents would tend to answer "no" or "unsure" while younger generations would say "yes," as Dyer found in 2011. The seventy-four fully participating respondents in 2020 showed no clear generational division on this question in the pre-survey results, suggesting either that older generations had grown more open to online community or else this specific group included a high concentration of older people inclined in that direction. In another positive sign, the percentage of participants calling online community "real" before the retreat increased comparably across generations when the post-retreat survey asked if they considered this particular faith-sharing retreat group in particular to be "real" community. One millennial even moved from "no" to "yes."

Question 16 showed the percentage of retreatants who felt comfortable sharing their faith with others online, as opposed to merely exchanging opinions. That percentage likewise increased across generations when asked after the retreat about their comfort with doing so in this group. Nevertheless, the successes reported in this chapter also reveal our retreat's limitations. People still felt less connected online than offline; young people remained few. Millennials were simultaneously the likeliest to change their religious habits and the scarcest retreatants. The next section unpacks what did not go as well as expected, especially with millennials.

What May Not Have Gone as Well as Expected

Some inherent limitations of my retreat's design necessarily constrain the conclusions of this final chapter, highlighting areas which did not succeed as well as hoped. Rather than reach out directly to the unaffiliated, I targeted self-identified believers with some degree of pre-existing religious observance and affiliation, following the apostolic insight that a committed group of disciples must be formed before reaching outside the circle of believers. Using the time-tested *Exercises* to help deepen their relationships conversationally, I hoped to form retreatants in the collaborative dialogue skills necessary to evangelize others effectively online. The primary limitations of this approach arose from my recruiting participants largely through *America's* Facebook page, an audience that skews toward older people with a pre-existing interest in Ignatian spirituality, and from the vertical focus of the *Exercises* on the relationship with God getting lost to some extent in the emphasis of the daily video prompts on horizontal faith-sharing. As a result, the retreat impacted older believers more than the coveted audience of younger disaffiliated Christians that chapters 1 and 2 discussed, making it more effective as a remote preparation for digital outreach than as an exercise of it.

For the sake of future learning and practice, it would be helpful to identify the ways in which some aspects of the retreat did not go as well as expected. Broadly, this Facebook group achieved a notable spirit of communion across generations in a way that simultaneously highlighted its dependence on an offline communal tradition (in this case, Ignatian spirituality, as presented by a trained Ignatian moderator who served in the role of retreat guide) to ground its online interactions. Despite this intergenerational spirit of communion, the survey responses highlight the ongoing challenge of reaching young people, who struggled in this retreat to maintain a group commitment with the regularity of older participants.

To what extent did this Facebook retreat group impact coveted millennials? As the last section indicated, it seems this group did largely integrate the twelve participating millennials with older generations in a common faith-based experience, but the small sample size and some lingering generational differences in the surveys make it hard to generalize many firm conclusions about them. Chapters 1 and 2 observed religious affiliation tends to decline and digital literacy to rise with each new Christian generation. That means a major goal of online religious outreach must be to form older participants in new forms of media interaction, preferably in contact with younger participants who for their part will grow in traditional Catholic wisdom. To that end, I found that older participants, especially among the majority Boomers, grew in comfort with online faith-sharing. But I did not so clearly identify the positive effects of their interaction on millennials and post-millennials.

Question 3 of the post-retreat survey found that older generations reported logging in more often than younger cohorts, a result that group conversations suggested may have been partly due to the greater free time that retired and coronavirus-isolated elders enjoyed. It may also have been partly due to the differently religious and unpredictable media habits of millennials, qualities which defy the easy categorizations of traditional indicators. I noticed older members of the Facebook group tended to participate at fixed times each day; younger members logged on at unpredictable intervals to view and discuss multiple days' videos at once. This result implies that the retreat's asynchronous design may hold promise for future interactions: As a middle ground compromise for both sides of the digital divide, the choice of Facebook for both videos and faith-sharing threads instead of Zoom (the live-time, scheduled extreme suggested by some older participants) or Instagram (the randomized, asynchronous extreme proposed by some younger participants) facilitated a reasonably interactive exchange broadly accessible to all ages. At the same time, these clashing generational styles of participation defy any attempt to judge one as better than the other, since participants of all ages reported positive experiences of the group regardless of whether they scheduled their logins or joined in at irregular intervals.

Based on the relatively small number of millennials who stayed for the whole retreat, it remains impossible to say how this asynchronous flexibility impacted those who did not finish. As a result, I was unable to conclude anything definitive about methodology other than asynchronous presentation was a reasonable compromise between the competing values of younger participants who desired flexibility to participate spontaneously and older retreatants who preferred fixed meeting times with live video interaction. Synchronous presentation might have had clearer values, but not for everyone in every age group.

Looking at the ideas of chapters 3 and 4 in terms of generations, it will now be possible to conclude that the easiest cohort for this Facebook group to reach were English-speaking Baby Boomers, mostly women, with a pre-existing interest in Ignatian spirituality. The hardest to reach were younger internet users, men, people without a pre-existing interest in Catholicism or Ignatian spirituality, and people living in non-English-speaking countries. With only twelve millennials completing the retreat and surveys, I left with more questions than answers about certain generational tensions. On the issue of shifting their atttitudes and habits toward a point of religious conversion, for example, a willingness to change their religious behavior was clearer among younger participants than older ones. Question 7 showed that larger percentages of younger respondents pledged to participate "more often" in religious activities offline and online after the retreat, whereas older members proved most likely to do so "about the same as always." This suggests older retreatants sought confirmation of their existing faith commitments more than outright conversion, a valid outcome envisioned by the *Exercises* that nevertheless did not intersect with younger members who sought greater personal change.

The fact that the two oldest generations reported the most "more than once a week" participation in offline and online religious events before the retreat suggests they felt less need to change in this area of religious participation. But the greater willingness of millennial participants to change their faith practices suggests that more participants from this generation may bear encouraging fruit. Additionally, the paradoxes of millennial experience that chapter 1 sketched remained present in other areas, not yielding any clear successes. For example, millennials reported the most neutral feelings about social media on question 8 of the pre-retreat survey, despite the report in chapter 1 that they use it the most of any generation in existing research. Asked about their satisfaction with the use of Facebook for this faith-sharing retreat, a larger percentage of participants from the oldest two generations reported on question 8 of the post-retreat survey feeling "highly satisfied" with using Facebook for this group than the percentage who described social media as "highly important" to them before it. Older generations evidently experienced a bigger shift from negative expectations of social media to positive experiences of the Facebook group than millennials.

Because of the limited sampling of millennials, the presence of only one post-millennial, and the failure of the surveys to envision these paradoxical outcomes, the retreat also generated scarce data to draw many firm conclusions comparing the generations to each other. Befitting their respective strengths, I might simply conclude that millennials entered the retreat with more fixed attitudes about their social media habits and Boomers with more fixed attitudes about their faith habits. It might also be said that the older generations, while not desiring strongly to change their religious habits, shifted their attitudes about digital media in ways that more clearly contributed to group unity on some points.

On some other aspects of spiritual growth, the millennials nevertheless hinted at stronger spiritual growth than older participants. In question 14 on the retreat outcomes, the twelve millennial survey respondents reported the highest percentage of any generation to receive the grace of a deeper relationship with God. This also made them the only age group where more people connected on a deep level with God through the Facebook group format than reported seeking this outcome before the retreat. That represents a notable exception to the general conclusion that on this retreat respondents connected more readily with each other, and perhaps with themselves, than with God. Perhaps millennials had God less in mind before the retreat, allowing them more room to grow in this area just as they desired to attend religious activities more often afterwards.

Millennials also reported themselves as the most willing to participate in more online faith-sharing groups through *America Media*, with around 90 percent of this generation (11 out of 12 respondents) saying "yes" on question 15 of the post-retreat survey. Older generations, despite leaving the retreat with a more positive experience of the digital group and an increased willingness to share faith online, seemingly departed with greater desires to share faith offline than to continue participating in online faith-sharing groups. On this point, the retreat may have moved some retreatants in different directions, deepening their generational tendencies rather than overcoming them. More specifically, it remained unclear whether younger participants overcame their well-researched generational mistrust of older authority figures in a way that made Boomers' online interactions with them an unqualified positive outcome, since the small number of millennials made it impossible to discern a desire to evangelize their peers flowing out of the example of their interactions with older participants.

As suggested earlier, many of the retreatants' before and after survey results support my conclusion that Facebook helped all generations grow more comfortable about sharing faith with people of different backgrounds in an online retreat setting. Since no generational differences arose in the last four questions of the surveys, which addressed the particular graces of each week of the *Exercises,* unity-in-diversity would seem to describe the particular outcomes of each seven-day session as well. In their exchanges around the subject matter of the four weeks of the *Exercises*, the narrative in chapter 3 showed older participants sharing the wisdom of their past experience and younger participants sharing more current struggles. But at the same time, all generations struggled equally to receive the graces of each session, making it impossible to conclude much of anything about the specific goals and outcomes for each weeklong session of the *Exercises*. Besides the notable increase in a common desire to suffer with Jesus on the cross that chapter 4 reported for the third week, perhaps reflective of the painful isolation that all participants shared in their Covid-19 quarantines, respondents' sense of receiving the graces of the other three weeks dropped from before to after the thirty-day retreat, denoting a weakened sense of connection to God. This might speak to the limitations of the way of putting religious questions that the *Exercises* imposed on the retreat, insofar as St. Ignatius employs assumptions which challenge contemporary sentiments.

It might seem like this retreat's focus on reaching Catholics in various stages of affiliation succeeded more clearly at forming older retreatants in digital discipleship than at strengthening the faith bonds of large numbers of younger retreatants through the communal spiritual tradition of the *Exercises*. Several older respondents shared their offline wisdom and experience of Ignatian retreats during the online discussion in ways that younger newcomers to the *Exercises* vocally appreciated; there were just too few millennials and too few clearly secularized participants to foster any deep conversations about obstacles to faith. The group did help Catholics of varied affiliations deepen their faith and learn Ignatian prayer tools to share it with others more effectively; it just focused more on older people who already had some grounding in these areas than on younger people who did not.

This reality does not diminish the positive experiences that retreatants spoke of in chapter 3 and the surveys that were analyzed in chapter 4: the formation of older disciples to interact more easily with younger people on their native soil of social media remains a success worth duplicating in future online faith-based groups. It simply shows the limited generalizations and conclusions that can be made because the participants came largely from a distinct community, in this case *America Media*. Because the group drew from *America's* regular media consumers, it included a majority of older, religious, educated women with an Ignatian interest, and few millennials and Generation Z. This is not a criticism of *America*. I conclude, though, that future online retreats will likely benefit from engaging millennials not already involved with *America*—something that *America* may wish to consider in of its future strategy, since translating Ignatian spirituality for larger numbers of young people could bring them more into an active faith within the orbit of Catholic media online.

Conclusion

Ten Research-Based Tips for Digital Outreach

The unintended outcomes in this retreat underline the ongoing need to find more creative ways to evangelize religious outsiders through social networking, accompanying them conversationally in charity and empathy. Emerging adults increasingly excel at digital interaction but have not learned the art of spiritual conversation necessary to develop their faith. No matter what believers do for them online, it remains better to do something than nothing. Yet Catholics, mindful of digital trends, must continue to evolve beyond simply posting YouTube videos and presuming that viewing them online is the same as participating in a retreat. Creating ever more interactive ways in which younger generations can both deepen faith and share it will be important. To better reflect this participatory theology of social communications, this final section will suggest additional adjustments to this retreat for future groups, ensuring a fuller communal witness to disaffiliated emerging adults.

A Facebook group and the *Exercises* remain sound elements through which retreatants of all generations reported having a positive experience. The *Exercises* provided a serviceable framework for the group's sharing of faith in Christ, Cardinal Francis Arinze's definition of evangelization mentioned in chapter 1. Future repetitions of online retreats like this, however, should recruit in other Facebook groups where young people hang out, including secular groups, and consider expanding beyond Facebook to emerging platforms that will grow in popularity over time. This more complex outreach will require moderators to join such groups and platforms, and begin to discern how they might be the most fruitful places of encounter. In the fast-moving world of social media, even the recent data in these chapters will soon constitute only one current in the ever-flowing stream of participatory media trends. Ongoing initiatives will also have to adapt traditional Catholic spirituality like that of the *Exercises* in ever more-creative ways. One ongoing challenge will be including older Catholics—as chapters 1 and 2 showed the need for more settled believers to model and invite younger people into the faith group they represent—in a way that does not drive off less religious emerging adults. Figuring out how to invite the right mix of participants will require experimentation, so as to reach fruitfully into the digital enclaves of millennials who operate well beyond traditional Catholic social networks.

The surveys will need to be refined. This tweaking will include finding better ways to help participants articulate their takeaways from the retreat. The relationship with God is a subtle aspect of spirituality that the existing survey questions in this retreat did not capture; future surveys might refocus the outcomes for each of the sessions around how participants influence each other as older-younger conversation partners and as peers. The process and means of digital evangelization in itself need to be discussed. For now, Facebook remains the largest social media site, but that will change as newer platforms like Instagram continue to grow and reshape human interactions.

I learned that sustained and serious online effort can have a more measurable impact on behavior and attitudes in interpersonal exchanges than in a personal sense of connection to a higher power. In an age of personal isolation the relational dimension of conversion should be examined carefully. I found that when Catholics engage in a digital faith-sharing community for an intensive period of retreat, they can develop the common experiences and knowledge necessary to lead such groups themselves. Future surveys might identify additional expectations related more specifically to this formation and how it can be used.

Time will always constrain Catholic social media outreach, since newcomers must spend many hours honing the digital literacy needed to lead or participate effectively in a moderated group like this *Spiritual Exercises* retreat. At the same time, when people have used Catholic digital platforms without proper moderation or without suitable reflection material, toxic culture war encounters have flared up rather than evangelization. Social media calls out for intentional leadership by digital disciples who exemplify selfless charity in accompanying others to new frontiers, zeal to discuss the essentials of faith in a unifying but challenging spiritual framework like that of the *Exercises*, and a desire to collaborate online as part of a group. In 2014 Daniella Zsupan-Jerome, a theologian and former media consultant to the US bishops, noted that the Pauline image of many parts united in one body will become a visible and convincing online witness if more and more Catholics willingly embrace a shared responsibility to communicate: "The digital presence of the Church likewise needs a unifying foundation, an element that moves these parts from interconnectedness toward an expression of communion."[141]

---

141. Daniella Zsupan-Jerome, *Connected Toward Communion: The Church and Social Communication in the Digital Age* (Collegeville: Liturgical Press, 2014), 127.

Regarding the radical change of life or the strengthening of existing vocational commitments that evangelization traditionally invites in texts like the *Exercises*, there seem to have been some positive results in terms of personal conversion, but, with reference to the Ignatian theme of each week, I can only conclude from this experience that during the retreat people's expectations changed from when they began. Their more "God-focused" language before the retreat seems to have become more "group focused" in the post-retreat survey. In other words, vertical expectations became horizontal interactions. This is not a bad outcome because I had hoped that Catholics would be able to interact in positive, respectful, and affirming ways. This retreat showed that such life-sustaining interaction is possible online, a particularly hopeful sign amid the fairly divisive exchanges on social media that remain commonplace even among self-identified Catholics today.

To conclude this story of digital evangelization, let me reiterate my group's partial success in addressing the sweeping concerns that underlie this case study. Chapter 1 surveyed secular media research to justify shifting from a packaged to a participatory media culture that engages emerging generations of digital natives. Outlining the pastoral crisis that sociologist Christian Smith sees in the breakdown of intergenerational faith transmission, exacerbated by the digital age, the first chapter set up the survey in chapter 2 of magisterial literature and of post-conciliar papal invitations to shift to a participatory style of ecclesial communication that moves from proclamation to conversation. The ideas of *communio*, synodality, and New Evangelization provided theological grounding for this faith-sharing group to engage in the individual participants' relationships with God, others, and themselves via the Ignatian Spiritual Exercises. Chapter 3 described Lonergan's notion of a shift of consciousness as the pastoral methodology for the relational spiritual growth envisioned in the design and implementation of this collaborative initiative aimed largely at existing members of *America's* Facebook groups. Chapter 4 then presented the survey results, setting up this final chapter's conclusions and recommendations.

This retreat showed overall that, whatever reluctance Catholics might have in sharing faith, getting the opportunity to do so online can increase their capacity for such interchange. The retreat's attempt to support this growth, rooted in Ignatian spiritual foundations and offering a big draw to the *America Media* consumers who participated, was far from perfect. Yet the basic experience of retreatants growing comfortable with spiritual conversation in the online group, deepening their interaction as they evolved intentionally into a smaller core of seventy-four participants, highlighted some key findings of these chapters. Digital evangelization can be effective when believers shift their mindset beyond the individualized consumption of prepackaged audiovisual prayer material to a more conversational approach that seeks to nurture communal religious experiences. As chapter 1 reported, Smith found parents who discuss faith with their children in a Catholic environment do better at passing it on, witnessing to the power of faith-sharing to influence young people.

This retreat supports the premise that Catholics can grow in their capacity to share faith through a method of dialogue. On social networks, the solution to Catholicism's generational crisis of disaffiliation may be found in evangelizing communities of discipleship who promote an interactive spirit of inclusivity that extends a spirit of hospitality to outsiders. In a participatory approach to Catholic media, dialogue partners work together as part of a team for the common good, allowing the fruits of their personal prayer to flow out to others online.

The final adjustment I would suggest for retreats like this, then, evokes the first proclamation of the early evangelists: Share the Good News. Nothing substitutes for the active, joyful, and selfless desire to accompany people, whether online or offline, by all means possible. No digital outreach will succeed without a firm decision to support people's spiritual growth charitably as they strive to deepen their relationships with God, one another, and themselves. People go online to seek connection. Online interaction by itself does not give them loving relationships with others, but it can extend and reflect the state of a faith community's offline unity in diversity, and that can be a very positive influence when digital disciples do it in an intentional way that brings others closer to God. For too long, Catholics in particular have been behind the digital curve. But if twelve apostles could start a global religious movement, perhaps the ongoing efforts to immerse believers as digital disciples in the story of evangelization may help renew it.

Bibliography

Church Documents

Benedict XVI. Address of His Holiness Pope Benedict XVI *Opening of the Pastoral Convention of the Diocese of Rome on the Theme: "Church Membership and Pastoral Co-Responsibility."* May 26, 2009. Holy See. http://w2.vatican.va/content/benedict-xvi/en/speeches/2009/may/documents/hf_ben-xvi_spe_20090526_convegno-diocesi-rm.html.

————. Apostolic Letter in the Form of *Motu Proprio Ubicumque et Semper* of the Supreme Pontiff Benedict XVI Establishing the Pontifical Council for the New Evangelization. Sept. 21, 2010. Holy See. http://w2.vatican.va/content/benedict-xvi/en/apost_letters/ documents/hf_ben-xvi_apl_20100921_ubicumque-et-semper.html.

————. Encyclical Letter *Deus Caritas Est* [God is Love]. Dec. 25, 2005. Holy See. http://w2.vatican.va/content/benedict-xvi/en/encyclicals/documents/hf_ben-xvi_enc_20051225_deus-caritas-est.html.

————. Encyclical Letter *Caritas in Veritate* [Charity in Truth]. June 29, 2009. Holy See. http://w2.vatican.va/content/benedict-xvi/en/encyclicals/documents/hf_ben-xvi_enc_20090629_caritas-in-veritate.html.

————. Post-Synodal Apostolic Exhortation *Verbum Domini* [On the Word of God in the Life and Mission of the Church]. Sept. 30, 2010. Holy See. http://w2.vatican.va/content/benedict-xvi/en/apost_exhortations/documents/hf_ben-xvi_exh_20100930_verbum-domini. html.

————. *Truth, Proclamation and Authenticity of Life in the Digital Age* [Message of His Holiness on the 45th World Communications Day]. June 5, 2011. Holy See. http://w2.vatican.va/ content/benedict-xvi/en/messages/communications/documents/ hf_ben-xvi_mes_20110124_45th-world-communications-day.html.

Burns, J. Patout, and Gerald M. Fagin, SJ, eds. *The Holy Spirit*. Eugene: Wipf and Stock Publishers, 2002.

Congregation for the Doctrine of the Faith. *Doctrinal Note on Some Aspects of Evangelization.* Oct. 6, 2007. Holy See. http://www. vatican.va/roman_curia/congregations/cfaith/ documents/rc_con_cfaith_doc_20071203_nota-evangelizzazione_en.html.

Congregation for the Doctrine of the Faith. *Letter to the Bishops of the Catholic Church on Some Aspects of the Church Understood as Communion.* May 28, 1992. Holy See. http://www.vatican. va/roman_curia/congregations/cfaith/documents/rc_con_cfaith_doc_28051992_communionis-notio_en.html.

Francis. Apostolic Exhortation *Gaudete et Exultate* [On Holiness in Today's World]. March 19, 2018. Holy See. http://w2.vatican.va/content/francesco/en/apost_exhortations/documents/ papa-francesco_esortazione-ap_20180319_gaudete-et-exsultate.html.

———. Encyclical Letter *Fratelli Tutti'* [On Fraternity and Social Friendship]. Oct. 3, 2020. Holy See. http://www.vatican.va/content/francesco/en/encyclicals/documents/papa-francesco_20201003_enciclica-fratelli-tutti.html.

———. Encyclical Letter *Laudato Si'* [On Care for Our Common Home]. May 24, 2015. Holy See, http://w2.vatican.va/content/francesco/en/encyclicals/documents/papa-francesco_20150524_enciclica-laudato-si.html.

———. Post-Synodal Apostolic Exhortation *Amoris Laetitia* [The Joy of Love]. March 19, 2016. Holy See. https://w2.vatican.va/content/dam/francesco/pdf/apost_exhortations/documents/papa-francesco_esortazione-ap_20160319_amoris-laetitia_en.pdf.

———. Post-Synodal Apostolic Exhortation *Christus Vivit* [Christ is Alive]. March 25, 2019. Holy See. http://w2.vatican.va/content/francesco/en/apost_exhortations/documents/papa-francesco_esortazione-ap_20190325_christus-vivit.html.

———. Post-Synodal Apostolic Exhortation *Evangelii Gaudium* [The Joy of the Gospel]. Nov. 24, 2013. Holy See. https://w2.vatican.va/content/francesco/en/apost_exhortations/ documents/papa-francesco_esortazione-ap_20131124_evangelii-gaudium.html.

———. *We Are Members One of Another (Eph 4:25): From Social Network Communities to the Human Community* [Message of His Holiness on the 53rd World Communications Day]. Jan. 24, 2019. Holy See. http://w2.vatican.va/content/francesco/en/messages/ communications/documents/papa-francesco_20190124_messaggio-comunicazioni-sociali.html.

John Paul II. Apostolic Pilgrimage to Poland, *Holy Mass at the Shrine of the Holy Cross, Homily of His Holiness John Paul II.* June 9, 1979. Holy See. http://w2.vatican.va/content/john-paul-ii/en/homilies/1979/documents/hf_jp-ii_hom_19790609_polonia-mogila-nowa-huta.html.

—————. Apostolic Pilgrimage to Central America, *Apostolic Address of the Holy Father John Paul II to the Assembly of CELAM.* March 9, 1983. Holy See. https://w2.vatican.va/content/ john-paul-ii/es/speeches/1983/march/documents/hf_jp-ii_spe_19830309_assemblea-celam.html.

—————. Encyclical Letter *Redemptoris Missio* [Mission of the Redeemer]. Dec. 7, 1990. Holy See. http://w2.vatican.va/content/john-paul-ii/en/apost_constitutions/ documents/hf_jp-ii_apc_15081990_ex-corde-ecclesiae.html.

—————. Post-Synodal Apostolic Exhortation *Christifideles Laici* [On the Vocation and the Mission of the Lay Faithful in the Church and in the World]. Dec. 30, 1988. Holy See. http:// w2.vatican.va/content/john-paul-ii/en/apost_exhortations/documents/hf_jp-ii_exh_30121988_christifideles-laici.html.

—————. Post-Synodal Apostolic Exhortation *Ecclesia in America* [On the Encounter with the Living Jesus Christ: The Way to Conversion, Communion and Solidarity in America]. Jan. 22, 1999. Holy See. http://w2.vatican.va/content/john-paul-ii/en/apost_exhortations/ documents/hf_jp-ii_exh_22011999_ecclesia-in-america.html.

Loyola, St. Ignatius. *The Spiritual Exercises of St. Ignatius: Based on Studies in the Language of the Autograph.* Translated by Louis J. Puhl, SJ. Chicago: Loyola Press, 1951. Also available online at http://spex.ignatianspirituality.com/SpiritualExercises/Puhl

Paul VI. Post-Synodal Apostolic Exhortation *Evangelii Nuntiandi* [On Evangelization in the Modern World]. Dec. 8, 1975. Holy See. http://w2.vatican.va/content/paul-vi/en/apost_exhortations/documents/hf_p-vi_exh_19751208_evangelii-nuntiandi.html.

Second Vatican Council. Decree *Ad gentes* [On the Mission Activity of the Church]. Oct. 11, 1962. Holy See. http://www.vatican.va/archive/hist_councils/ii_vatican_council/documents/ vat-ii_decree_19651207_ad-gentes_en.html.

Second Vatican Council. Decree *Apostolicam actuositatem* [On the Apostolate of the Laity]. Nov. 18, 1965. Holy See. http://www.vatican.va/archive/hist_councils/ii_vatican_council/ documents/ vat-ii_decree_19651118_apostolicam-actuositatem_en.html.

————. Decree *Inter Mirifica* [On Social Communications]. Dec. 4, 1963. Holy See. http:// www.vatican.va/archive/hist_councils/ ii_vatican_council/documents/vat-ii_ decree_19631204_inter-mirifica_en.html.

————. Dogmatic Constitution *Lumen gentium* [On the Church], Nov. 27, 1964. Holy See. http://www.vatican.va/archive/hist_councils/ii_vatican_council/documents/vat-ii_const_19641121_lumen-gentium_en.html.

United States Conference of Catholic Bishops. *Go and Make Disciples: A National Plan and Strategy for Catholic Evangelization in the United States.* Nov. 18, 1992. http:// www.usccb.org/beliefs-and-teachings/how-we-teach/evangelization/go-and-make-disciples/introduction_go_and_make_disciples.cfm.

————. *Living as Missionary Disciples: A Resource for Evangelization.* Washington, DC: United States Conference of Catholic Bishops, 2017.

Secondary Resources

Anderson, Keith. *The Digital Cathedral: Networked Ministry in a Wireless World.* New York: Morehouse Publishing, 2015.

Anderson, Keith, and Elizabeth Drescher. *Click2Save Reboot: The Digital Ministry Bible.* New York: Church Publishing, 2018.

Arinze, Francis Cardinal. *The Evangelizing Parish.* San Francisco: Ignatius Press, 2018.

Barron, Robert. *Arguing Religion: A Bishop Speaks at Facebook and Google.* Park Ridge: Word on Fire, 2018.

————. *Renewing Our Hope: Essays for the New Evangelization.* Washington, DC: The Catholic University of America Press, 2020.

Baym, Nancy. *Personal Connections in the Digital Age.* Cambridge: Polity Press, 2015.

Center for Applied Research in the Apostolate, Georgetown University. "Catholic New Media Use in the United States, 2012." November 2012. http://www.usccb.org/about/communications/upload/Catholic_New_Media_Use_in_United_States_2012.pdf.

Dees, Jared. *To Heal, Proclaim, and Teach: The Essential Guide to Ministry in Today's Catholic Church.* Notre Dame: Ave Maria Press, 2016.

Dulles, SJ, Avery Cardinal. *Evangelization for the Third Millennium.* New York: Paulist Press, 2009.

Dyer, John. *From the Garden to the City: The Redeeming and Corrupting Power of Technology.* Grand Rapids: Kregel Publications, 2011.

Fisichella, Rino. *The New Evangelization: Responding to the Challenge of Indifference.* Leominster, England: Gracewing, 2012.

Hennessy, Brittany. *Influencer: Building Your Personal Brand in the Age of Social Media.* New York: Citadel Press, 2018.

Jenkins, Henry, Mizuko Ito, and Dana Boyd. *Participatory Culture in a Networked Era.* Cambridge: Polity Press, 2018.

Landry, Scot. *Transforming Parish Communications: Growing the Church Through New Media.* Huntington: Our Sunday Visitor, 2014.

Massaro, SJ, Thomas. *Mercy in Action: The Social Teachings of Pope Francis.* Lanham, Maryland: Rowman & Littlefield, 2018.

McCarty, Robert J. and John M. Vitek. *Going, Going, Gone: The Dynamics of Disaffiliation in Young Catholics.* Winona, MN: Saint Mary's Press, 2017.

O'Collins, SJ, Gerald. *Rethinking Fundamental Theology: Toward a New Fundamental Theology.* Oxford: Oxford University Press, 2011.

Orsy, SJ, Ladislas. *Receiving the Council: Theological and Canonical Insights and Debates.* Collegeville: Michael Glazier, 2009.

O'Toole, SJ, Robert F. *Who Is a Christian? A Study in Pauline Ethics.* Eugene: Wipf & Stock, 1990.

Pew Research Center. "Religion and Electronic Media: One-in-Five Americans Share Their Faith Online." Nov. 6, 2014. https://www.pewforum.org/2014/11/06/religion-and-electronic-media/.

———. "In U.S., Decline of Christianity Continues at Rapid Pace." Oct. 17, 2019. https:// www.pewforum.org/2019/10/17/in-u-s-decline-of-christianity-continues-at-rapid-pace/?fbclid=IwAR3UPLL91PSTQfwNgNiTjetu5wYjBuQBXZL8DCD-fN-vBoMg7shn3Jd_d9YU.

Rivers, CSP, Robert S. *From Maintenance to Mission: Evangelization and the Revitalization of the Parish.* New York: Paulist Press, 2005.

Smith, Christian, Kyle Longest, Jonathan Hill, and Kari Christoffersen. *Young Catholic America: Emerging Adults In, Out of, and Gone from the Church.* Oxford: Oxford University Press, 2014.

Wittberg, SC, Patricia. *Catholic Cultures: How Parishes Can Respond to the Changing Face of Catholicism.* Collegeville: Liturgical Press, 2016.

Zech, Charles, Mary L. Gautier, Mark M. Gray, Jonathon L. Wiggins, and Thomas P. Gaunt, SJ, *Catholic Parishes of the 21st Century.* New York: Oxford University Press, 2017.

Zsupan-Jerome, Daniella. *Connected Toward Communion: The Church and Social Communication in the Digital Age.* Collegeville: Liturgical Press, 2014.

Tertiary Resources

Al-Amodi, Sarah. "Collaborate Online As a Small Group." *Education for Primary Care* 26, no. 2 (2015): 127-129. https://doi: 10.1080/14739879.2015.11494327.

Cerveny, Caroline. "Digital Disciple Network." Digital Disciple Network. Accessed November 10, 2019. https://digitaldisciplenetwork.wordpress.com/.

Chesterton, Gilbert Keith. "What's Wrong with the World." 1910. In *The Wisdom of Mr. Chesterton: The Very Best Quotes, Quips, & Cracks,* edited by Dave Armstrong. Charlotte: Saint Benedict Press, 2009.

DeSiano CSP, Frank P. *Reactivating Our Catholic Faith: Reflections to Get Real About Faith.* New York: Paulist Press, 2009.

Dimock, Michael. "Defining Generations: Where Millennials End and Post-Millennials Begin." *Fact Tank: News in the Numbers.* March 1, 2018. http://www.pewresearch.org/fact-tank/2018/03/01/defining-generations-where-millennials-end-and-post-millennials-begin/.

Gray, Mark M. "New Poll: 36 Percent of Young Catholics Say They Will Attend Mass Less Often After Pandemic." *America: The Jesuit Review.* September 14, 2020. https://www.americamagazine.org/faith/2020/09/14/poll-catholics-attend-mass-less-often-covid-19.

Goggins, Sean P., James Laffey, and Michael Gallagher. "Completely Online Group Formation and Development: Small Groups as Socio-Technical Systems." *Information Technology & People* 24, no. 2 (June 2011): 104-133. https://doi: 10.1108/09593841111137322.

Hamann, Kerstin, Philip H. Pollock, and Bruce M. Wilson. "Assessing Student Perceptions of the Benefits of Discussions in Small-Group, Large-Class, and Online Learning Contexts." *College Teaching* 60 (2012): 65-75. https://doi: 10.1080/87567555.2011.633407.

Jahng, Namsook. "Collaboration Indices for Monitoring Potential Problems in Online Small Groups." *Canadian Journal of Learning and Technology* 39, no. 1 (Winter 2013): 2-16. https://doi: 10.21432/T2Z30Q.

Lewis, Bex. "The Digital Age: A Challenge for Christian Discipleship?" Unpublished paper presented at The Proceedings of the European Conference on Social Media, July 2014.

Lipka, Michael. "Millennials Increasingly Are Driving Growth of 'Nones.'" Pew Research Center (May 12, 2015). https://www.pewresearch.org/fact-tank/2015/05/12/millennials-increasingly-are-driving-growth-of-nones/.

Makitalo-Siegl, Kati. "From Multiple Perspectives to Shared Understanding: A Small Group in an Online Learning Environment." *Scandinavian Journal of Educational Research* 52, no. 1 (February 2008): 77-95, https://doi: 10.1080/00313830701786677.

Mielach, David. "Gen Y Seeks Work-Life Balance Above All Else." *Business News Daily* (March 30, 2012). https://www.businessnewsdaily.com/2278-generational-employee-differences.html.

Reznich, Christopher B. and Elizabeth Werner. "Facilitators' Influence on Student PBL Small Group Session Online Information Resource Use: A Survey." *BMC Medical Education* 4, no. 1 (15 June 2004): 1-5. https://doi: 10.1186/1472-6920-4-9.

Shearer, Brady. "5 Research-Backed Reasons Millennials Are Done With Church." *Pro Church Tools.* Aug. 16, 2017. https://prochurchtools.com/millennials-stop-attending-church/.

Twenge, Jean M. "Have Smartphones Destroyed a Generation?" *The Atlantic.* September 2017. https://www.theatlantic.com/magazine/archive/2017/09/has-the-smartphone-destroyed-a-generation/534198/.

White, Christopher. "Study Finds Young Strong in Faith Amid Virus, But Increasingly Lonely." *Crux.* April 20, 2020. https://cruxnow.com/church-in-the-usa/2020/04/study-finds-youth-strong-in-faith-amid-virus-but-increasingly-lonely/.

Methodology

Barry, SJ, William A., and William J. Connolly, SJ. *The Practice of Spiritual Direction.* New York: HarperOne, 2009.

Bevans, SVD, Stephen B., *Models of Contextual Theology,* 2nd ed. Maryknoll: Orbis Books, 2002.

Lonergan, SJ, Bernard J.F. "Dimensions of Meaning." 1965. In *The Lonergan Reader,* edited by Mark D. Morelli and Elizabeth A. Morelli. 387–401. Toronto: University of Toronto Press, 1997.

————. *Insight: A Study of Human Understanding.* New York: Harper and Row, 1978.

————. *Method in Theology.* Toronto: University of Toronto Press, 1990.

Lowney, Chris. *Heroic Leadership: Best Practices from a 450-Year Old Company That Changed the World.* Chicago: Loyola Press, 2003.

————. *Pope Francis: Why He Leads the Way He Leads.* Chicago: Loyola Press, 2013.

Loyola, St. Ignatius. *The Spiritual Exercises of St. Ignatius of Loyola: With Points for Personal Prayer from Jesuit Spiritual Masters.* Edited by Sean Salai, SJ Charlotte: TAN Books, 2020.

McLuhan, Marshall. *Understanding Media: The Extensions of Man,* 3rd Edition. Edited by W. Terrence Gordon. Berkeley: Gingko Press, 2003.

McLuhan, Marshall, and Quentin Fiore. *The Medium is the Massage: An Inventory of Effects.* Berkeley: Gingko Press, 1967.

Tetlow, SJ, Joseph A. *Making Choices in Christ: The Foundations of Ignatian Spirituality.* Chicago: Loyola Press, 2008.

Topical Timeline of Retreat Videos

Pre-Retreat Invitation, Discernment, and Orientation Period: August 30-September 30

August 30
The moderator creates the "Spiritual Exercises Faith-Sharing Retreat Group" and shares invitation text with a link to the Facebook group in existing *America* groups as well as two other Ignatian groups; he posts the Survey Monkey link to the pre-retreat questionnaire on the group page and pins it under the "Announcements" section.

August 31
The moderator posts a welcome note with instructions to complete the survey. Participants begin a daily practice of conversing and interacting with him and with each other about the topic and their experience of this Facebook format in the comment box below the video.

September 1-7
The moderator posts a short video each day reading through his historical preface to his edition of the *Spiritual Exercises*, section by section, and engages in conversation with participants in the comment box below videos as a template to follow. He announces that daily videos will be posted each morning sometime before noon US Central Standard Time, with guided reflection and faith-sharing prompts to journal and then share about in the comment box.

September 8
Introductory video on the Anima Christi (Soul of Christ) prayer reprinted at the front of most editions of the *Spiritual Exercises.*

September 9
Introductory video on common traditional prayers used during the *Exercises.* The moderator begins sharing short introductions and reflection

questions from his book, inviting participants to post their response to the prompts in the comment box below each video starting this day.

September 10
Introductory video posted on spiritual reading (or movies) to help focus during the *Exercises.*

September 11
Introductory video presents St. Ignatius's "Rules for Eating" (SpEx #210).

September 12
Video presents St. Ignatius's own introduction to the *Exercises,* the 20 introductory annotations (#1-20) which open the book.

September 13
Video presents the premise of the *Exercises* that St. Ignatius shares in his subtitle (#21) to the title of the book following his introduction.

September 14
Video presents the presupposition of the good that St. Ignatius articulates (#22) not only as a basis for charitable interactions between retreatants and their spiritual guides, but as a reminder to presume charitable intentions from others in general as a matter of etiquette.

September 15
Video presents the brief catechesis on morals (#32) that St. Ignatius provides for the First Week to help retreatants reflect on how to redirect their thoughts, words, and actions toward God.

September 16
Introductory video presents the recommendations of St. Ignatius for general confession and communion during the First Week (#44) for those so moved to this form of self-reflection.

September 17
Introductory video presents the meditation on hell (#65) as a sample of the topics St. Ignatius presents during the First Week, discussing a template for how faith-sharing retreat will proceed.

September 18
Video presents a reflection on God's love for sinners with a brief note from #71 of the *Exercises,* to be elaborated and repeated October 7 with a meditation on death at the end of the first week.

September 19

Introductory video presents additional recommendations St. Ignatius offers (#73) to help retreatants enter more deeply into prayer interiorly and exteriorly during the First Week.

September 20

Video presents the Rule of Penance St. Ignatius offers (#82) as his tenth additional recommendation for the First Week to guide retreatants seeking to practice more disciplined habits of eating, sleep, and other ascetical topics.

September 21

Video presents the First Week Rules for the Discernment of Spirits (#313) that St. Ignatius offers to help retreatants discern what comes from God and what comes from somewhere else in moments of consolation, desolation, and dryness in prayer.

September 22

Video presents the Application of Senses (#121) that St. Ignatius proposes as a method for using the sight, sound, smell, touch, and taste to reflect more affectively on the mysteries of the life of Jesus starting in Week Two.

September 23

Video presents the Second Week Recommendations (#127) St. Ignatius offers to help people shift from reflecting on human brokenness and God's love in Week One to reflecting on the life of Jesus beginning in Week Two.

September 24

Video presents introductory comments of St. Ignatius to discerning a vocation or state of life (#135) starting in the Second Week. Moderator reminds people that they may take what they like and leave the rest from these introductory videos, perhaps even returning to them as relevant during the retreat itself in October.

September 25

Video presents the Second Week Rules for Discernment of Spirits (#328) aimed particularly at helping people who face challenges after making inital progress in the spiritual life.

September 26

Video presents the reflection of St. Ignatius on the three kinds of people (#149) who respond to the call to follow Jesus in very different ways.

September 27
Video presents the thoughts of St. Ignatius on perfecting a state of life already chosen (#189) by finding a vocation within one's vocation, making a decision about how to live out a lifelong choice more intentionally each day in smaller ways.

September 28
Introductory video presents the simple meditation points which St. Ignatius offers in an appendix on the Mysteries of the Life of Our Lord (#261) which retreatants pray over in the Bible.

September 29
Video presents some introductory comments of Fr. Charles De Place, the original French-language translator and editor of this edition of the *Exercises,* to the Third Week theme of suffering with Jesus during the retreat.

September 30
Video presents some introductory comments of Fr. Charles De Place, the original French-language translator and editor of this edition of the *Exercises,* to the Fourth Week theme of rejoicing with the risen Jesus during the last session of the retreat. Moderator also announces that the group has officially gone "secret" by becoming hidden as well as private in preparation for the 30-day retreat beginning the next day.

First Session:
Week 1 of the Spiritual Exercises, October 1-7

October 1
First Principle and Foundation (SpEx #23) and suggested readings: Lk 6:30-33; *The Imitation of Christ* Book 3 chapters 9, 22, and 26.

October 2
Particular Examen (#24) and suggested passage: Mt 25:1-31; *Imitation of Christ* Book 1 chapters 21, 22; Book 2 chapter 6; Book 4 chapter 7.

October 3
General Examen (#43) and suggested reading: 2 Cor. 2: 7-9.

October 4
First Exercise on Sin (#45) and suggested passage: Ps 139 (Lord You Search Me and You Know Me).

October 5
Second Exercise on Sin (#55) and suggested reading: Lk 12:33-43

October 6
Third Exercise on Sin (#62) repetition of last two days and suggested readings: Rev. 3; Imitation of Christ Book 3 chapter 14.

October 7
Other Exercises: On My Death (#71) and suggested readings: Mt 25:31-46 and Imitation of Christ Book 3 chapter 14.

Second Session:
Week 2 of the Spiritual Exercises, October 8-14

October 8
Call of the King (#91) bridge exercise into Week 2 and suggested readings: Jn 15; Col. 3; Imitation of Christ Book 3 chapters 13-32.

October 9
Exercise on the Incarnation (#101) and suggested readings: Lk 1:26-56; Imitation of Christ Book 2 chapters 1, 7, and 8.

October 10
Exercise on the Nativity (#110) and suggested readings: Lk 2:1-21; Imitation of Christ Book 3 chapters 1, 2, and 18.

October 11
Exercise on the Hidden Life of Jesus (#132-134) and suggested readings: Lk 2:40-52, Imitation of Christ Book 1 chapter 20; Book 3 chapters 44 and 53.

October 12
Exercise on the Two Standards (#136) and suggested readings: Mt 19; Imitation of Christ Book 3 chapters 23, 27, 31, and 56.

October 13
Three Kinds of Humility (#165) and suggested readings: Mt 10; Imitation of Christ Book 1 chapters 15-16; Book 3 chapter 4

October 14
Making a Choice of a Way of Life (#169) and suggested readings: Jn 1; Lk 5; Mt 4; Mk 1; Imitation of Christ Book 3 chapter 54.

Third Session:
Week 3 of the Spiritual Exercises, October 15-21

October 15
Palm Sunday (#287) and suggested readings: Mt 21: 1-11; Mk 11:1-10; Lk 19:29-44; Jn 12:12-19.

October 16
Jesus preaching in the Temple (#288) and suggested reading: Lk 19:47-48.

October 17
Exercise on the Eucharist (#190) and suggested readings: Mt 26: 17-30; Imitation of Christ Book 4 chapters 1-2.

October 18
From the Last Supper to the Agony in the Garden (#200) and suggested readings Mt 26:31-46; Mk 14:27-42; Lk 22:24-46; Jn 13:31-38, 14-17, 18:1-2.

October 19
From Pilate to the Crucifixion (#296) and suggested readings: Mt 27:31-38; Mk 15:20-28; Lk 23:24-38; Jn 19:12-24.

October 20
The Death of Jesus (#297) and suggested readings: Mt 27:39-56; Mk 15:29-41; Lk 23:39-49; Jn 19:25-39.

October 21
The Burial of Jesus (#298) and suggested readings: Mt 27:57-66; Mk 15:42-47; Lk 23:50-56; Jn 19:30-42.

Fourth Session:
Week 4 of the Spiritual Exercises, October 22-28

October 22
Jesus Appears to His Mother (#218 and 299).

October 23
Second Apparition of the Risen Christ (#300) with suggested readings: Mt 28:1-7; Mk 16:1-11; Lk 24:1-11; Jn 20:1, 11-18.

October 24
Eighth Apparition of the Risen Christ (#306) with suggested reading: Jn 21:1-25.

October 25
Ninth Apparition of the Risen Christ (#307) with suggested readings: Mt 28:16-20; Mk 16:14-20; Lk 24:46-53.

October 26
The Ascension of Jesus Christ (#312) with suggested readings: Acts 1:1, 11.

October 27
Contemplation to Attain the Love of God (#230) and suggested readings: Jn 17; 1 Jn 4; Imitation of Christ Book 3 chapters 5, 6, and 34.

October 28
Second Way of Prayer with the Our Father (#249) guided *lectio divina* method.

End of Retreat Transition Days:
October 29-30

October 29
Rules for the Distribution of Alms (#337) reflecting on how to serve the poor after retreat.

October 30
Rules for Thinking with the Church (#352) reflecting on belonging to the Catholic community and request to do post-group survey in Survey Monkey link pinned to announcements page.

Post-Retreat Days to Complete Survey:
October 31-November 7

October 31
Farewell and thank you video, invitation to keep using group, heads-up to watch for more *America* faith-sharing groups, and reminder to submit post-group survey from Survey Monkey that will remain pinned to the top of the announcements page for next seven days until November 7 as people running a few days behind on the asynchronous videos finish the retreat.

Pre-Survey and Post-Survey of Retreat Participants

Pre-Retreat Survey Results

▶ **Q1:** This anonymous survey asks questions about your background, online experiences, and religious habits. By continuing with this survey, you agree to participate in a 30-day online retreat faith-sharing group based on the Spiritual Exercises of St. Ignatius and hosted on Facebook in connection with America Media, as well as to complete a survey about your experiences after it concludes. If you select "no" in response to this first question, please do not complete the rest of the survey that follows, but submit it with only the first question completed.

ANSWER CHOICES	RESPONSES	
Yes, I am willing to participate	100.00%	74
No, I am not willing to participate	0.00%	0
TOTAL		74

▶ **Q2:** In which generation were you born?

ANSWER CHOICES	RESPONSES	
1901-1927 ("Greatest Generation")	0.00%	0
1928-1945 ("Silent Generation")	8.11%	6
1946-1964 ("Baby Boomers")	50.00%	37
1965-1980 ("Generation X")	24.32%	18
1981-1996 ("Generation Y"/"Millennials")	16.22%	12
1997-2012 ("Generation Z"/"iGeneration")	1.35%	1
TOTAL		74

▶ **Q3:** Where do you live?

ANSWER CHOICES	RESPONSES	
United States of America and territories	82.43%	61
Elsewhere in North America/Central America	6.76%	5
South America	0.00%	0
Europe	4.05%	3
Asia	5.41%	4
Africa	0.00%	0
Australia or New Zealand	1.35%	1
Antarctica	0.00%	0
TOTAL		74

▶ **Q4:** How would you describe your current religious affiliation?

ANSWER CHOICES	RESPONSES	
Catholic (including the Eastern Catholic churches)	91.89%	68
Eastern Orthodox Christian	1.35%	1
Protestant (including Anglican Communion)	4.05%	3
Jewish	0.00%	0
Muslim/Islamic	0.00%	0
Nothing in Particular (Atheist, Agnostic, or "None")	0.00%	0
Other (please specify)	2.70%	2
TOTAL		74

Other: Questioning to former Catholic recently attending American Baptist services; Indigenous

▶ **Q5:** How strongly do you feel personally connected to a particular faith-based community?

ANSWER CHOICES	RESPONSES	
A lot	71.62%	53
Some	18.92%	14
A little	6.76%	5
Not at all	2.70%	2
TOTAL		74

▶ **Q6:** How strongly do you feel personally connected to a Higher Power as you understand it?

ANSWER CHOICES	RESPONSES	
A lot	87.84%	65
Some	10.81%	8
A little	1.35%	1
Not at all	0.00%	0
TOTAL		74

▶ **Q7:** How often have you been involved in a religiously sponsored event (funeral, wedding, church service, online discussion, spiritual reading, prayer or meditation group, etc.) in the past 12 months? Select the response that most closely approximates your attendance.

ANSWER CHOICES	RESPONSES	
None	0.00%	0
1-6 times a year	13.51%	10
7-11 times a year	4.05%	3
Once a month	4.05%	3
2-3 times a month	9.46%	7
Once a week	24.32%	18
More than once a week	44.59%	33
TOTAL		74

▶ **Q8:** How important is online interaction (e.g., Instagram, Facebook, comment boxes, other social media platforms) in your life?

ANSWER CHOICES	RESPONSES	
Highly Important	21.62%	16
Important	52.70%	39
Neutral	22.97%	17
Unimportant	2.70%	2
Highly Unimportant	0.00%	0
TOTAL		74

▶ **Q9:** How much, if at all, have you shared your faith with others online during your life?

ANSWER CHOICES	RESPONSES	
A lot	36.49%	27
Some	36.49%	27
A little	21.62%	16
Not at all	5.41%	4
TOTAL		74

▶ **Q10:** How much, if at all, have you shared your faith with others offline (face-to-face) during your life

ANSWER CHOICES	RESPONSES	
A lot	54.05%	40
Some	37.84%	28
A little	8.11%	6
Not at all	0.00%	0
TOTAL		74

▶ **Q11:** What particular hopes or desires do you bring to this online faith-sharing experience? Please write them in the space below.

will deepen relationship God spiritual continue growing closer God hope grow learn structure love become community develop understand online share relationship God God welcome others spirituality faith deepen faith life grow hope journey experience interesting better idea time new feel prayer life group grow closer God help pray

Survey Monkey generated the above Word Cloud to summarize the results of this question. Seventy-two participants answered this free response question and two participants skipped it. Here is the full text of all 72 individual responses to question 11; all spelling and grammatical errors are original to the texts as respondents typed them out.

1.   Making some friends that support me on my path with God.

2.   I have felt very cut off from my faith during the pandemic—I had been meeting with a spiritual director and doing a nightly Examen, and I've fallen out of both habits.

3.   I pray that I will grow to live a more Christ-like life. I wish to live out the demands of the Gospel more radically.

4. Build more knowledge about my faith and understand how to keep it vivid day to day.

5. To grow closer to God

6. This is my first online experience of this type. I am typically reserved at first until i understand where others are in their journey.

7. I hope to grow more sensitive to Jesus' presence in my life, and to develop a stronger and more fruitful habit of prayer.

8. Taking time to get closer to Jesus so that I can follow his path. Loving and helping others.

9. I hope to deepen my faith & feel a connection to other like minded ppl. Because of Covid, I have not been participating in mass in person & feel disconnected from others.

10. I'm not exactly sure, but a friend told me about it and thought it might be helpful for me. I think it will be interesting to see what others share too.

11. I desire to be more bold with my faith and to have courage without fear in sharing the truth of our identities as sons and daughters of God.

12. I want to bring myself into a more intimate relationship with God to better understand and follow His will and to feel his love and guidance in the remainder of my life

13. Deepening my relationship with God

14. Finding peace of mind

15. Increase my faith

16. To have a deeper sense of spirituality. To feel closer to God. To learn how to really pray.

17. A deepening of faith

18. Become a better person and a better Catholic.

19. Continued growth in my relationship with God and to walk with others in their quest.

20. I am interested to hear about others' experiences of faith, as well as increasing my knowledge of foundational truths taught by the Church fathers.

21. I hope to grow closer to God and feel part of a community. I have not attended mass since March because of the pandemic and I feel disconnected from my faith

22. To rediscover God's love for me. To understand a bit more as to why so many unfortunate events and plans have failed to better my life.

23. I like to listen to others and their spiritual experiences. I think when we share we are more inclined to open up about our beliefs to others. I'm looking for community with other believers.

24. Get some good spiritual advice and time to reflect on my faith.

25. I am interested in Ignatian insights as to how to handle everyday life - grew up in a very Jesuit influenced household

26. Spiritual growth

27. I always appreciate an opportunity to grow in my faith and make more room for God in my life, and I love faith sharing groups. Covid has made it tough to gather in groups, so I love the idea of moving that online.

28. A more regular prayer life that is more structured.

29. Developing a practice that's regular.

30. I am seeking a disciplined way to incorporate prayer into my life. I have too many excuses to not pray...they are GOOD excuses :)

31. A new retreat experience Some group discussion Finally participating in an Ignatian experience. Maybe some insight to break thru to a little more trust

32. Deepen my spirituality, improve my behavior, love more, forgive more, treat and heal intergenerational trauma, be a better helper to others, help heal this sick society

33. I hope grow in faith, hope and charity and better be able to see Christ in others. I would like to have a deeper relationship with Jesus. I am also interested in hearing about how others experience their faith journey.

34. A stronger understanding of my faith.

35. I hope to enhance my understanding of, and participation in, the Spiritual Exercises and sharing in prayer, comments and fellowship with fellow participate.

36. Getting more involved with God and my relationship with him

37. A connection with other people. A deepening of my spiritual life

38. I would like to develop a new spiritual practice in a community. I would like to learn more about the examin.

39. To grow in wisdom and knowledge of God. To learn new ways to pray and to meet other people who also want to know God more deeply.

40. To become more connected to God through the spiritual exercises and the online community.

41. I welcome the structure of being a part of a larger group, and therefore have an appointment with a daily spiritual practice. But whatever I gain from others in the group is pure bonus!

42. I hope to become closer to God. I like the idea of some more structure in my faith life in order to help me do that. I am excited to be a part of this experiment.

43. Deepen my faith journey during this COVID-19 pandemic when it isn't possible in my state to attend weekly mass in person and receive the Eucharist.

44. At this time, my life is in transition. In the past year I have lost some dear friends, sold my home (where I lived for over fifty years), moved into an small apartment where I have been isolated as is the rest of the world for the last six months. My hope is that I can use this experience to deepen my faith.

45. 1. I hope to resolve my discouragement with the Roman Catholic Church. 2. I hope to grow closer to God as some of my perceptions are changing. 3. I hope to find ways to conform my thoughts and behavior to be a more positive force in my family and community.

46. That I become closer to my faith. I feel I am strong, but do not meditate often enough. I think participating in this will help me with that.

47. My hope is to find a space that fosters spiritual growth while helping me connect with others who have a similar appreciation for the role of discernment in spirituality.

48. I am hoping to get some clarity and to feel God's support during these very difficult time.

49. hope to become a part of something again, to belong. Being in isolation has changed me

50. To walk a journey with others. To help with discernment. To deepen my relationship with God

51. Family Diversity Faithful Citizenship (would like to pray more about it)

52. Sharing within a community. I live alone and private on-line sharing is often the only channel open to me

53. I am looking forward to exchanging ideas and thoughts on ways to remain connected to my faith. My Jesuit experience at Holy Cross was pivotal for me to continue my faith. And I desire a community of those who understand Jesuit theology.

54. Get and be closer to God, prepare me to see and be with Him when I depart this world.

55. I hope to know more about my Faith and be closer to God

56. Commitment to a more consistent prayer life and in exploring what the Exercises will reveal at this time in my life.

57. It's been a long time since my last retreat so I'd like to get all possible benefits.

58. Growth in relation with Creator, Life Sustainer God Life Force

59. Interest, Understanding, Open-mindedness

60. I would love to continue growing in my relationship with God. Perhaps this experience will help me find other ways to pray.

61. Reconnect with my Church, especially now. Grow my spiritual life. Learn how to share in a "welcoming" way (welcoming from me, welcome to others)

62. I miss retreats

63. I hope to grow deeper in my spirituality

64. I wish to establish a regular prayer life. I am a graduate of a Jesuit University and attend a Jesuit Parish at Boston College, MA.

65. opportunity to explore Ignatian Spirtuality in-depth within a group setting (versus trying to learn it on my own)

66. To continue to grow in my acceptance and realization of God's love for me. To engage in faith sharing with a larger community than my neighborhood parish. To continue growing and experiencing Ignatian spirituality.

67. To explore Ignatian spirituality

68. My hope and desire is to come closer to my God and my brothers and sisters. To embrace the differences and to understand with more enlightenment the path I am on.

69. Deeper relationship with God.

70. Draw closer to God. Receive guidance. Learn in order to share.

71. deepen my relationship with God; gain insights/ideas from others (as well as share them); consider new ideas/interpretations

72. Nourished prayer life; faith translated into action

▶ **Q12:** How often, if ever, does it occur to you to discuss faith-based content on Facebook?

ANSWER CHOICES	RESPONSES	
Always	6.76%	5
Usually	22.97%	17
Sometimes	41.89%	31
Rarely	18.92%	14
Never	9.46%	7
TOTAL		74

▶ **Q13:** Do you consider online community to be a type of "real" community?

ANSWER CHOICES	RESPONSES	
Yes	55.41%	41
No	6.76%	5
Unsure	37.84%	28
TOTAL		74

▶ **Q14:** What outcome would you like to see from this online faith-sharing group? Please choose all that apply

ANSWER CHOICES	RESPONSES	
A better relationship with God	82.43%	61
Stronger sense of connection to a faith-based community	66.22%	49
More knowledge about Catholic teachings	47.30%	35
More knowledge about Ignatian spirituality	74.32%	55
Unsure	1.35%	1
Other (please specify)	4.05%	3
Total Respondents: 74		

▶ **Q15:** How many of the people you know online also play a role in your offline life outside of the internet?

ANSWER CHOICES	RESPONSES	
A lot	29.73%	22
Some	45.95%	34
A few	18.92%	14
None at all	5.41%	4
TOTAL		74

▶ **Q16:** How comfortable do you feel with talking about your personal faith and religious experiences, as opposed to exchanging opinions, in an online faith-sharing group?

ANSWER CHOICES	RESPONSES	
A lot	33.78%	25
Some	44.59%	33
A little	21.62%	16
Not at all	0.00%	0
TOTAL		74

▶ **Q17:** To what extent does this statement accurately describe your spiritual life? Statement: "I have a deeply felt sense of God's love for me even though I am a sinner."

ANSWER CHOICES	RESPONSES	
Very Much	69.86%	51
Somewhat	24.66%	18
Not Much	4.11%	3
Not At All	0.00%	0
Unsure	1.37%	1
TOTAL		73

▶ **Q18:** To what extent does this statement accurately describe your spiritual life? Statement: "I feel a desire to accompany Jesus and labor with him in his ongoing ministry."

ANSWER CHOICES	RESPONSES	
Very Much	74.32%	55
Somewhat	22.97%	17
Not Much	2.70%	2
Not At All	0.00%	0
Unsure	0.00%	0
TOTAL		74

▶ **Q19:** To what extent does this statement accurately describe your spiritual life? Statement: "I feel like I have suffered with Jesus on the cross."

ANSWER CHOICES	RESPONSES	
Very Much	16.22%	12
Somewhat	54.05%	40
Not Much	17.57%	13
Not At All	9.46%	7
Unsure	2.70%	2
TOTAL		74

▶ **Q20:** To what extent does this statement accurately describe your spiritual life? Statement: "I feel like I have rejoiced with the risen Lord, Jesus Christ, in gratitude for all he gives me."

ANSWER CHOICES	RESPONSES	
Very Much	51.35%	38
Somewhat	36.49%	27
Not Much	10.81%	8
Not At All	0.00%	0
Unsure	1.35%	1
TOTAL		74

Post-Retreat Survey Results

▶ **Q1:** This survey asks questions about your experience of the online faith-sharing group, based on the 30-day Spiritual Exercises of St. Ignatius retreat, that you recently completed through the collaboration of America's Facebook page. By continuing with this survey, you confirm that you logged into the faith-sharing group at least once. If you filled out the pre-survey and agreed to the study, but did not end up logging into the group to participate, please select "no" here and scroll to the end to submit this survey without answering any of the other questions.

ANSWER CHOICES	RESPONSES	
Yes, I will take this survey because I logged into the faith-sharing group at least once	100.00%	74
No, I will not take this survey because I didn't actually log into the faith-sharing group	0.00%	0
TOTAL		74

▶ **Q2:** In which generation were you born?

ANSWER CHOICES	RESPONSES	
1901-1927 ("Greatest Generation")	0.00%	0
1928-1945 ("Silent Generation")	8.11%	6
1946-1964 ("Baby Boomers")	50.00%	37
1965-1980 ("Generation X")	24.32%	18
1981-1996 ("Generation Y"/"Millennials")	16.22%	12
1997-2012 ("Generation Z"/"iGeneration")	1.35%	1
TOTAL		74

▶ **Q3:** On average, how often did you log on to this Facebook faith-sharing group each week?

ANSWER CHOICES	RESPONSES	
More than once a day	9.46%	7
Once a day	29.73%	22
A few times a week	48.65%	36
Weekly	6.76%	5
Less than weekly	5.41%	4
TOTAL		74

▶ **Q4:** How would you describe your current religious affiliation?

ANSWER CHOICES	RESPONSES	
Catholic (including the Eastern Catholic churches)	91.89%	68
Eastern Orthodox Christian	1.35%	1
Protestant (including Anglican Communion)	4.05%	3
Jewish	0.00%	0
Muslim/Islamic	0.00%	0
Nothing in Particular (Atheist, Agnostic, or "None")	0.00%	0
Other (please specify)	2.70%	2
TOTAL		74

"Other" responses: Soon to be former Catholic leaning towards American Baptist; Indigenous

▶ **Q5:** How strongly did you feel personally connected to this online community during the 30 days of faith-sharing?

ANSWER CHOICES	RESPONSES	
A lot	29.73%	22
Some	41.89%	31
A little	24.32%	18
Not at all	4.05%	3
TOTAL		74

▶ **Q6:** How strongly did you feel personally connected to a Higher Power as you understand it during the 30 days of faith-sharing?

ANSWER CHOICES	RESPONSES	
A lot	77.03%	57
Some	13.51%	10
A little	9.46%	7
Not at all	0.00%	0
TOTAL		74

▶ **Q7:** How often do you intend to attend a religiously sponsored event (funeral, wedding, church service, online discussion, spiritual reading, prayer or meditation group, etc.) moving forward from this faith-sharing group into the future?

ANSWER CHOICES	RESPONSES	
More often than I did before this faith-sharing group	34.25%	25
About the same as I always do	65.75%	48
Less often than I did before the group	0.00%	0
I don't plan to attend religious services in the future	0.00%	0
TOTAL		73

▶ **Q8:** This online retreat utilized Facebook. How satisfied do you feel about the use of Facebook to facilitate the group interactions?

ANSWER CHOICES	RESPONSES	
Highly Satisfactory	36.49%	27
Satisfactory	36.49%	27
Neutral	20.27%	15
Unsatisfactory	6.76%	5
Highly Unsatisfactory	0.00%	0
TOTAL		74

▶ **Q9:** How likely are you to discuss faith-based content with others online as you move forward from this faith-sharing group into the future?

ANSWER CHOICES	RESPONSES	
More often than I did before this faith-sharing group	39.19%	29
About the same as I always do	59.46%	44
Less often than I did before the group	1.35%	1
I don't plan to share my faith online in the future	0.00%	0
TOTAL		74

▶ **Q10:** How likely are you to discuss faith-based content with others offline (face-to-face) moving forward from this online faith-sharing group?

ANSWER CHOICES	RESPONSES	
More often than I did before this faith-sharing group	43.24%	32
About the same as I always do	56.76%	42
Less often than I did before the group	0.00%	0
I don't plan to share my faith offline in the future	0.00%	0
TOTAL		74

▶ **Q11:** What particular hopes or desires did you find were fulfilled in this experience? write them in the space below.

learning connection God also strengthen Jesus Deepening love practicing able connected faith closer God prayer Lord helped connection hoped spiritual exercises experience relationship God God grow retreat Ignatian Spirituality life way wanted deeper found prayer life understanding God s better hope feel time day helpful community desires fulfilled exercises Learn St Ignatius desire spiritual

Survey Monkey generated the above Word Cloud to summarize the results of this question. Seventy-two participants answered this free response question and two participants skipped it. Here is the full text of all 72 individual responses to question 11 arranged generationally; all spelling and grammatical errors are original to the texts as respondents typed them out.

195

Silent Generation (5 respondents)

1. To include my faith focus/awareness more in my life each day
2. A greater sense of connection to God's presence. A creative sense of peace with events in my life
3. This experience helped me to review my spiritual life: my beliefs, my understandings, my practices. It also helped me to re-commit in necessary ways.
4. I was looking for a period of introspection and rest
5. The desire to pray more. The desire to be more reflective in my prayer and faith life. The desire to become a more holy person, more in love with God and to live more aware of God' presence in my life.

Baby Boomers (37)

6. To step back and take stock. To be more aware of God's presence. To see a way through sin.
7. It was a powerful online experience
8. I was exposed to tools that have helped me enter more deeply into my relationship with God. New ideas from Fr. Sean, the daily exercises and the comments of others provided feedback that expanded my understanding. Also, with Covid and the decrease in personal interaction it was perfect to have this online retreat. And for me personally I live in what's been called "mission territory" for the church so there are very few opportunities in my community to have Catholic sponsored religious discussions, retreats, classes, etc. I am very grateful that I found this site online and was able to participate.
9. A more extensive understanding of the *Exercises.*
10. It gave me the incentive to stop in the midst of my day and pray. Sounds simple, but it's not always easy to do. This retreat was a gift in the midst of my too busy life.
11. Didn't really have any hopes or desires fulfilled in this experience.
12. I was focused and committed to my prayer time for the duration of the experience.
13. Much better st mindful meditation. Loved being lead and learning how to enter the silence better.
14. I learned to make some reflections and prayers...
15. I had wanted to do a 30 day retreat since the early 90s when I worked at Gonzaga but never had the time and then we moved out of the area and did not have opportunity. I was pleasantly surprised by the depth of sharing from the participants and the creation of a solid, if narrowly focused community. Each day we were able to come to this sacred space.

16. Spiritual growth and confirmation of my faith and belief system.

17. I was interested in the introduction to *The Imitation of Christ*, and the *Spiritual Exercises*.

18. I came into the retreat with three goals. I've been doing spiritual reading, but it contained lots of theology, and the theology had me in my head, instead of in my heart. The Ignatian Spirituality helps with that. I'm anxious to let go of my ego and discover more of who I am in God. I don't know that the retreat did anything directly with that, but it did leave me more open to God. I went in with lots of questions about sin, and the first week helped with some of that.

19. I hoped to understand my Catholic faith and the writings of St Ignatius more clearly. I also wanted to know myself better. These hopes and desires were fulfilled.

20. Learn more about St. Ignatius. Hear more thoughts of Christ from other Christians. Share in our faith and beliefs. Grow more in my connection with Christ.

21. I drew closer to God, I forgave someone having better connected with my own sinfulness. I lived the Scriptures and was given direction through the colloquys. I feel more loved by Him and I love Him more, particularly through his suffering and the Hope I found.

22. I expected to hear Father talking live online about our faith. There were connection problems, so my hopes were not always fulfilled. I expected to hear thoughts and opinions from other people. There were not a lot of them.

23. The hope to remain focused during prayer. The guided contemplations were very helpful for this. I hoped to start and finish the retreat which i did. When i did [t]he spex years ago i remember skimming over week 3 whereas this time i was able to stay with it. I usually attend daily mass but due to covid this and examen were alternative moments

24. I am happy to have learned about St. Ignatius. My wife and I are making more of an effort to watch uplifting videos on saints. We have enjoyed these before but they are now more frequent in our life. I hope this will continue to grow and develop even greater spiritual thirst in our lives.

25. I was interested to see how it would work online compared to individuals in with guided as I am at present studying.

26. I wanted to deepen and expand my personal prayer life, and I was curious about the Exercises. I feel that my prayer life has been renewed, and that when I pray now I am less distracted and more engaged in prayer.

27. I experienced some of the exercises, which I'd always been curious about. Also, I'd hoped to draw closer to God and break through a problem, and that occurred. I feel better able and willing to follow God's will in this challenge with a sense of certainty.

28. I'd hoped to find peaceful reflection and a deeper connection with my faith.

29. God stirs my heart in the midst of lockdown - with no in-person sacraments, or for this experience, no in-person discussions with the retreat master, yet still God spoke. What an awesome God!

30. Learning about new ways that I can practice using to actually feel Jesus' reality as a human, and thereby feel God's guidance more strongly in decisions on how to live my life.

31. Closer to God, by speaking to him in moments set aside each day to do so.

32. I had hoped to learn more about Ignatian Spirituality and was happy to do that. I also found my experience of God in my life strengthened by using my imagination, my senses to enhance my prayer life in this and other devotions.

33. I was just hoping to connect with Our Lord and His people again. I have been so isolated, as has everyone else.

34. I thought it was remarkable that I was discovering ways to include Jesus in my daily life. The thought of "hating sin" had never entered my mind. I had never sat at the foot of the Cross watching Christ die. I have noticed that reading scripture has become mysterious to me, the words have their own life and I'm more willing to reread in an effort to understand.

35. I desired to enter into meditative/contemplation daily. This retreat has helped me begin to do this.

36. Ability to participate in the spiritual exercises. Would not have been able to do so otherwise

37. I felt closer to God, more aware of His Divine Providence. I deep more confident in discerning God's will & learned more about praying the Lectio Divina.

38. I wanted to reestablish a habit of daily prayer. I wanted to clarify where I was in my spiritual understandings . I wanted to discern if I was ready to move on spiritually. This really helped

39. Feeling connected to a faith community during the pandemic. Learning more about St Ignatius. Growing deeper in my Faith

40. Happiness

41. It caused me to re-examine the [tenets] of my faith and recommit my life to Jesus Christ

42. It was so so helpful in strengthening my connection to God, especially when I am away from my parish life of being in community. I had hoped for that this might happen. The retreat gave me structure and suggestions of what to consider in my relationship with God and the Church. The private site was a very good idea. I felt free to express where I was and it was nourishing and enlightening to read where others were.

Generation X (18)

43. Made the EE accessible

44. I've wanted to do an Ignatian retreat for a while, but logistics made it not possible for me to do. I appreciated this opportunity but found it difficult to keep up with it every day. I made it through the first week only, but I hope to catch up with the other videos this month at my own pace.

45. I had hoped to find a way to participate in some form of the spiritual exercises.

46. I understand my current relationship with God and where I want to be..... I knew I needed a reboot and this helped!

47. I wanted to see what the long retreat was like. Now I have an idea about the content.

48. It was good to share reflections I found it helpful

49. God's Patience with me and his constant Love for me despite my weakness

50. A deeper relationship with God. Finding time to be present to God's daily blessings.

51. Learned about a new source for faith sharing

52. A sense of God's intimacy and an answer to something for my future development

53. I became more aware of what I need to work on to improve my relationship with God

54. A closer connection to my Lord and others in this community.

55. Connection to God, relationship with Jesus, better understanding of the exercises

56. I wanted to know what was a 30-day Spiritual Exercises retreat.

57. I had hoped to grow closer to God through the group. Unfortunately I was unable to participate as frequently as I'd hoped due to some challenges in my personal life.

58. I wanted to stay sane during COVID and remind myself to act as a person of faith

59. Received an introduction to the 30 day retreat as I wanted. I'd been exposed to Ignatian spirituality but this let me experience more of it. I also wanted to connect with my real-life friends and experience it together.

60. It was great that I did not have to leave my home and still be part of faith sharing and deepening my relationship with the Lord.

Millennials (11)

61. I met God through Father Salai's guidance :) and able to get closer to him

62. Understanding more about the Ignatian Spirituality

63. I have been practicing the Exercises by myself for many years, but do to funds, I never attended a retreat. I hope for many years to be able to experience a retreat such as this and found that hope and desire fulfilled. I enjoyed having a teacher and videos and not having to depend on myself and my translations of the meaning of the texts.

64. Deepening of prayer life

65. Knowing I'm not alone and others have similar situations and feeling as mine.

66. More at peace with Jesus' love for me.

67. Intimacy with the Lord. He took me deeper than I was expecting and allowed me to dream with Him.

68. Good to have a community and learn more about the spiritual Exercises—I would like access to the retreat so I can go back and listed to the weeks again. My participation was interrupted when people close to me where had covid... so I did not participate for some time so I got really behind—but I think the meditations would be really useful still as I slowly start tagging back up

69. I was able to grow in and strengthen my life of prayer, grow in my reliance on God's grace, and grow in my ability to discern God's providential guidance. Prayer, learning to be sustained by God and depending on His grace, and growing in the ability to discern His hand more clearly is especially important when parish life, access to the sacraments, and community are so limited.

70. I loved the Ignatian style of meditations, using my imagination to establish the scenes from Scripture, and to hold colloquies at the end of a day. Doing these—especially the composition of place and seeing Jesus in my imagination— helped me to feel closer to Jesus than I usually do. It had a real affective impact on me and I felt an increase of love for God in my heart. My desire to actually spend more time in prayer, and my desire to feel closer to God, were both fulfilled.

71. I got a peak of Ignatian Spirituality

Generation Z (1)

72. When I did the sessions I felt more connected to God

▶ **Q12:** Other than Facebook, is there another digital media format you would suggest that America use for an online faith-sharing group? Please write your suggestion in the blank. If you do not write anything, your answer will be recorded as "no suggestion."

use website might retreat present found group social media worked

meeting Facebook community Zoom comments

suggestion Instagram people Twitter well need know Microsoft Teams

Maybe Youtube

Survey Monkey generated the above Word Cloud to summarize the results of this question. Fifty-six participants answered this free response question and 18 participants skipped it. Here is the full text of all 72 individual responses to question 12 arranged generationally; all spelling and grammatical errors are original to the texts as respondents typed them out.

Silent Generation (3)

1. YouTube
2. I have been using Zoom with a spiritual direction group. It works well.
3. ZOOM sessions.

Baby Boomers (28)

4. No Suggestion
5. Zoom
6. I don't know any other format. It worked for me because I have a Facebook account but something different might reach more people and include people who don't do Facebook.
7. Facebook is the only social media site I use.
8. I have found zoom to be a great platform as well.
9. I don't know digital media well enough to make any kind of suggestion!
10. No suggestion
11. Youtube
12. Zoom would allow real time interaction but also would restrict participation to those who could comply with that
13. WhatsApp, Google Meet, or Microsoft Teams.
14. No suggestion
15. Zoom day retreats Speakers to encourage us Debate forums

16. I would suggest breaking into small groups of maybe 6- 10 people with a set time weekly to meet and share. How about Zoom?

17. We use zoom for luve meetings but db is useful for referring to page in my own time and zone

18. Zoom could work but the flexibility would need to be present in that offering also since I was not able to watch the videos when they were presented live.

19. Cannot think of any

20. I've found Zoom to be very helpful. My anonymous group recently had a virtual convention. Some sessions were panelists only, but others were more interactive. Of course they were not asynchronous. but folks were present from all over the world. A previous convention had simultaneous translations in 5 languages.

21. None

22. Have you talked with any of the communities that host "closed" or "paying" membership who might be willing to have you provide this kind of retreat on their website? (e.g. http://www.icpe.org/; https://www.wordonfire.org/; https://franciscan.edu/; etc.)

23. FB is the platform I'm most comfortable, but younger folks probably are more comfortable with newer platforms that I'm unfamiliar with.

24. Twitter, if it could be a private group.

25. I'm not very tech savvy, so not aware of other options

26. Maybe a dedicated website, and not social media. I tend to get lost in the social media rabbit hole. No one's fault but my own. Use the social media to direct to the website

27. A directed Zoom room based on Ignatian prayer w a designated Ignatian spiritual director as the group leader.

28. Recorded WebEx or Microsoft teams might work yet I don't know if you can comment like we have done on Facebook

29. Facebook seems to be for older people. You had better interview the younger crowd to see what they are into.

30. Microsoft Teams, Zoom, Slack

31. I am not well versed in the scope of digital media. I like the opportunity for writing and reading comments in addition to hearing/seeing the retreat leader.

Generation X (15)

32. Mighty Networks or other community platform

33. I find it easier to be "present" when events are live.

34. Maybe a text messaging small group format

35. Maybe a zoom meeting for each time zone could help with connections in the secret group setting

36. Zoom or the like might encourage more interaction and might help create a sense of community.
37. Twitter
38. Not sure
39. No suggestion
40. Ascension Presents
41. Zoom
42. I think it needs to be "more" than Twitter or Instagram- but cannot be as much as Zoom... i.e. people need to be able to come and go as their schedule allows
43. No answer
44. This worked well
45. No
46. No suggestion

Millennials (9)

47. Youtube - General audi[e]nce Tiktok - Gen Z Instagram - Millenials
48. No suggestion
49. I wish I knew, I honestly don't like facebook that much, but don't know of any other solutions.
50. No suggestion.
51. I'm not a very techy person. But it was a little hard to interact with others on Facebook other than just commenting my answers and maybe reading someone else's.
52. I liked the recorded meditations—I just don't use Facebook as often. Not YouTube—I liked the community aspect on Facebook!
53. Having one's own site could be especially helpful especially if it had a "message board" where people could have ongoing discussions on topics that arise.
54. Instagram could work for a faith-sharing group structured around images (sacred art, architecture, etc) but Facebook worked really well for videos + participants interacting in comments.
55. No suggestion

Generation Z (1)

56. Slack, Discord

▶ **Q13:** Do you consider this Facebook faith-sharing group to have been a type of "real" community?

ANSWER CHOICES	RESPONSES	
Yes	58.11%	43
No	12.16%	9
Unsure	29.73%	22
TOTAL		74

▶ **Q14:** What outcomes did you see in your spiritual life at the end of this online faith-sharing group? Please choose all that apply

ANSWER CHOICES	RESPONSES	
A better relationship with God	68.49%	50
Stronger sense of connection to a faith-based community	28.77%	21
More knowledge about Catholic teachings	30.14%	22
More knowledge about Ignatian spirituality	91.78%	67
Unsure	5.48%	4
Other (please specify)	16.44%	12
Total Respondents: 73		

▶ **Q15:** Based on this experience, would you be interested in participating in another online faith-sharing group at the America Media Facebook page

ANSWER CHOICES	RESPONSES	
Yes	82.19%	60
No	1.37%	1
Unsure	16.44%	12
TOTAL		73

▶ **Q16:** How comfortable did you feel talking about your personal faith and religious experiences, as opposed to exchanging opinions, in this Facebook group?

ANSWER CHOICES	RESPONSES	
A lot	45.95%	34
Some	33.78%	25
A little	14.86%	11
Not at all	5.41%	4
TOTAL		74

▶ **Q17:** To what extent does this statement accurately describe the grace you received in Week One of the retreat? Statement: "I grew in a deeply felt sense of God's love for me even though I am a sinner."

ANSWER CHOICES	RESPONSES	
Very Much	50.00%	37
Somewhat	32.43%	24
Not Much	8.11%	6
Not At All	4.05%	3
Unsure	5.41%	4
TOTAL		74

▶ **Q18:** To what extent does this statement accurately describe the grace you received in Week Two of the retreat? Statement: "I grew in my desire to accompany Jesus and labor with him in his ongoing ministry."

ANSWER CHOICES	RESPONSES	
Very Much	51.35%	38
Somewhat	36.49%	27
Not Much	2.70%	2
Not At All	0.00%	0
Unsure	9.46%	7
TOTAL		74

▶ **Q19:** To what extent does this statement accurately describe the grace you received in Week Three of the retreat? Statement: "I experienced a stronger desire to suffer with Jesus on the cross."

ANSWER CHOICES	RESPONSES	
Very Much	32.43%	24
Somewhat	37.84%	28
Not Much	9.46%	7
Not At All	6.76%	5
Unsure	13.51%	10
TOTAL		74

▶ **Q20:** To what extent does this statement accurately describe the grace you received in Week Four of the retreat? Statement: "I rejoiced more deeply with the risen Lord, Jesus Christ, in gratitude for all he gives me."

ANSWER CHOICES	RESPONSES	
Very Much	51.35%	38
Somewhat	25.68%	19
Not Much	5.41%	4
Not At All	1.35%	1
Unsure	16.22%	12
TOTAL		74

New City Press

New City Press is one of more than 20 publishing houses sponsored by the Focolare, a movement founded by Chiara Lubich to help bring about the realization of Jesus' prayer: "That all may be one" (John 17:21). In view of that goal, New City Press publishes books and resources that enrich the lives of people and help all to strive toward the unity of the entire human family. We are a member of the Association of Catholic Publishers.

www.newcitypress.com
202 Comforter Blvd.
Hyde Park, New York

Periodicals
Living City Magazine
www.livingcitymagazine.com

Scan to join our mailing list for discounts and promotions or go to www.newcitypress.com and click on "join our email list."